CONSULTING 101

How to succeed as a training consultant

By Joel Gendelman

ASTD

AMERICAN SOCIETY
FOR TRAINING AND
DEVELOPMENT

1640 KING STREET
BOX 1443
ALEXANDRIA, VIRGINIA
22313-2043

703/683-8100
FAX 703/683-8103

CONSULTING 101

Ordering information: Books published by the American Society for Training and Development can be ordered by calling 703/683-8100.

This publication is designed to provide accurate and authoritative information in regard to the subject matter covered. It is sold with the understanding that the publisher and author are not engaged in rendering legal, accounting, or other professional advice. If legal advice or other expert assistance is required, the services of a competent professional should be sought. — *From a Declaration of Principles jointly adopted by a Committee of the American Bar Association and a Committee of Publishers*

Library of Congress Catalog Card Number: 95-077167

ISBN: 1-56286-019-4

Illustrations by Jim Paterson.

ASTD

AMERICAN SOCIETY
FOR TRAINING AND
DEVELOPMENT

1640 KING STREET
BOX 1443
ALEXANDRIA,VIRGINIA
22313-2043

703/683-8100
FAX 703/683-8103

CONTENTS

PREFACE

There's only one thing more painful than learning from experience, and this is not learning from experience.

—*Archibald MacLeish*

My journey into consulting started the same way it starts for many other training professionals. I began my career as a training practitioner and later became a training manager, director, and vice-president. One Friday afternoon, my boss told me that — because the firm I worked for had fallen on hard times — I was being laid off. After hearing this news, I figured that I had worked for other people long enough. I knew what I was doing and felt that it was time to make it on my own.

Over the next 15 years, I probably made every consulting mistake in the book (every mistake described in this book, anyway). I've written Consulting 101 to pass on some of the knowledge that I've gained to people, like you, who are considering consulting or just starting their own training consulting practices.

Since most people starting out have little time for theory, I've written this book to be as comprehensive, practical, and to the point as possible. And since we all need a little bit of humor in our lives — especially when we embark on a new journey — I have intentionally kept the tone light-hearted and conversational, so the book is enjoyable to read.

ACKNOWLEDGEMENTS

I would like to thank all those who have contributed to my development as a training consultant. Thanks to Roger Pell for opening my eyes to the art of selling. My warmest thoughts go out to Caroline Yeager and Sivasailam Thiagarajan (Thiagi) for their early appreciation and support of my work. I would also like to extend my sincerest gratitude to my mother, Lila Gendelman, who taught me the beauty of the written word, and to my father, Irving Gendelman, who introduced me to the excitement of business. And finally, loving thanks to my wife, Diane, and my children, Marc and Laurence, who continue to share with me the good times, the bad times, and all those times in between.

—*Joel.*

INTRODUCTION

Nearly everyone at one time or another entertains the idea of starting a business. In today's fast-paced business world, where change and job instability seem to be daily blue-plate specials, corporate trainers increasingly grapple with whether or not they should add the word entrepreneur to their resumes. But before you take the plunge into the sea of self-employment, you need to have a plan.

Reading *Consulting 101* is an excellent place to start. By sharing personal experiences and insights, I hope to help you understand what it takes to be a successful training consultant and to explain why it's worth the effort.

Section 1 describes the realities that must be considered by any person who is thinking of or actively planning to "go solo." There's good news and bad news, so brace yourself for some heavy soul-searching before you continue on to Section 2.

If your desire to become a consultant is still undaunted after reading the previous chapters, Section 2 provides practical steps and advice on how to proceed with establishing your business. Here chapters describe how to set up an office, secure clients, and run the day-to-day operations of a business. Section 3 explains how you can stay in business by marketing your services and building repeat business.

The book also provides valuable samples of introductory letters, written agreements, and checklists that you can adapt or use. It also features additional resources that you can use to continue your learning.

It's tough to get started as an independent training consultant. But with thorough planning, hard work, and the expertise that you already possess, you can enjoy the professional rewards and financial security you've always dreamed about.

SECTION 1: IS CONSULTING THE LIFE FOR YOU?

This section can help you decide if consulting is really for you by walking you through eight harsh realities of being a consultant. It also identifies the things you really need before you go out on your own, and describes key characteristics of successful consultants.

Chapter 1 What You Should Know Before Starting Out

Chapter 2 What's So Great About Consulting?

Chapter 3 When Do You Take the Plunge?

CHAPTER 1
What You Should Know
Before Starting Out

Consulting is one of the greatest professions. If you handle it right, you can live in that special corner of the world that you've dreamed about, do what you enjoy most, have more free time than you imagined possible, and make a good living while you're at it. But before you go ahead, quit your job, and hang a shingle on your spare-bedroom door, there are a few harsh realities that you should know about.

The Harsh Realities

Consider the following before you decide you want to be a consultant.

✔ **Reality 1: If you think working for someone else is precarious, try working for yourself.**

Most successful training consultants will tell you that they often have plenty of money and time, but rarely do they have both at the same time. While you're working on a project, life is champagne and caviar. When the project's over, it's a quick return to macaroni and cheese.

✔ **Reality 2: You're not going to get rich quick.**

Consultants at the top of the training profession earn a great deal. We often hear about such top earners as Tom Hopkins, author of *How To Master the Art of Selling*; Tony Robbins, motivational speaker, author, and star of info-mercials; and Ken Blanchard, coauthor of *The One-Minute Manager*, *Situational Leadership*, and *Raving Fans*, who command fees of $20,000 per day or more. Publicity about these famous people paints a distorted picture of how much most independent training consultants earn. In fact, the average training consultant's billing rate is less than $100 an hour.[1] If you consider expenses and the total number of non-billable hours you work, this adds up to a fairly modest wage. If you intend to be a successful consultant, you'd better be prepared to work hard.

✔ **Reality 3: Life isn't going to be easy.**

When you work for a large company, you're judged by your professional expertise. If you know your stuff, managers and co-workers usually look beyond your shortcomings. This changes, however, the moment you leave your corporate home to become an independent training consultant.

Your professional expertise remains a critical success factor because potential clients want to hire the training consultant with the highest levels of knowledge and skill. But think about how clients find consultants and assess their skills. Often the training consultant who gets the job is the one who has the best connections, uses the best marketing tools, and makes the most convincing presentations.

✔ **Reality 4: You'll starve waiting for the phone to ring.**

Once you leave corporate life, you'll be surprised how quickly your co-workers forget you. As a consultant, if you want to continue paying your bills and putting food on the table, you'll have to pick up the telephone and start "dialing for dollars." And that's just the beginning. Once you find prospective clients, it will probably take months of follow-up before you seal that first deal.

Some professionals are able to negotiate contracts with their former employers, but this arrangement is becoming increasingly rare. States are clamping down on the use of former employees as consultants or contractors, because many companies have misused such arrangements as a way to avoid payroll taxes. As a result, many corporations now have policies that prohibit hiring former employees as consultants.

If you expect to start your practice by working for your former (or soon-to-be-former) employer, find out what the company's policy is regarding using ex-employees as contractors. Even if there is a policy against hiring former employees, there may be a way around it if the company really wants to hire you. For example, if you aren't allowed to contract with the company directly, see if you can subcontract or be hired through a temporary agency.

✔ **Reality 5: Consultants are treated differently.**

Many potential clients see consultants as peddlers. Other people who claim qualifications similar to yours have knocked on their doors. Don't expect immediate respect. To make it through the first few months of marketing your services, you're going to need to develop a tough hide.

✔ Reality 6: You'll spend up to 50 percent of your time on non-billable work.

When starting your training consulting practice, you'll need to spend a great deal of time on marketing your services. Even after your practice is established, you'll have to continue your marketing efforts. I recommend no less than one day a week for such activities. And, of course, there will always be other non-billable tasks to do, such as paying bills, collecting fees, and struggling with a host of computer problems.

✔ Reality 7: You'll only get to keep half the money.

Supplies, telephone services, secretarial assistance, insurance, computers, and other equipment all cost money. Then taxes take their bite. Every practice is different, but a good rule of thumb is to expect that only half of the money that you take in will make its way into your pocket.

✔ Reality 8: You'll still have to do work that you don't like.

I hate accounting, but I do my own because I can't see paying a CPA to do what I can handle for free. I detest calling new prospects, but I can't find anyone who can market my practice as well as I can. If you're serious about succeeding, you'll find yourself doing lots of things that you don't like. But here's the upside. You're still the boss and at the end of each day you've built a little more of something that's truly yours.

What You Need in the Beginning

Before you rush to print up a stack of letterhead, make sure that you have the following:

■ Money in the bank or an "angel." As a new consultant, you'll need to spend several thousand dollars up front on computer equipment, business stationery, and telephone and delivery services before you earn a penny. Unless you've negotiated a contract with your former employer, you are well-connected, or you are extremely fortunate, you're going to need some "seed" money to cover your initial operating expenses. You're also going to need enough money to cover at least three months' worth of living expenses. For the latter, you may need to depend on a very special "angel." This angel is usually a spouse, significant other, parent, or wealthy relative who's willing to ride out the tough financial times with you.

■ **Adequate insurance coverage.** The price of health care is substantial. If you're married, your spouse may be able to include you on his or her health plan. If you're not married but live with someone, a handful of companies allow coverage of a "spousal equivalent."

The next best option is an affordable COBRA (Consolidated Omnibus Reconciliation Act) policy from your former employer. If this is not available to you, try getting a policy through an alumni or professional association. The latter may offer affordable disability and life insurance, too. Also check your home-owner's or renter's insurance to make sure that you have coverage for such essential equipment as your computer, printer, answering machine, and facsimile machine.

■ **A few good friends and contacts—or lots of guts.** You're going to have to get your first clients from somewhere. Starting from scratch by telephoning new people takes a relatively long time. The process of converting a "cold call" prospect into a client typically takes nine months to a year. An easier, quicker way to build your client base is through your current business associates and their network of contacts.

If you're new in town or don't have many contacts, join and become active in a local chapter of a professional training association, such as the American Society for Training and Development or the National Society for Performance and Instruction. If your training practice relates to a particular industry, also consider joining that industry's associations through their special interest groups for training. A partial list of professional training organizations appears in the back of this book.

What Really Makes a Successful Consultant

If you've faced the realities and have the basic resources, you're well on your way. Even so, you may not be ready for consulting. To succeed, you also need to have or develop these personal characteristics:

■ **Motivation and discipline.** When you work for yourself, no one is going to watch over you and make sure that you work. You can sleep in every day and know one will know. But eventually your creditors will know if can't pay your bills.

You should be at your desk for at least eight hours a day, five days a week, whether you have something billable to do or not. When you don't, spend your time doing something that will bring in billable work: make calls, send out mailings, or write an article.

■ **Strength and survival instincts.** Clients will not always be nice to you. In fact, some of them may be downright nasty. People and companies also are not always fair. But clients have every right to speak their minds about the projects that they're paying for—and they will. You'll need to have the strength and inner confidence to rise above these challenges, be gracious and, above all, leave it at the office where it belongs.

■ **Presence.** Clients get their first impression of you as you walk through the door, so you need to look good! That means dressing well, looking confident, and using the right handshake or greeting. My recommendation is to watch others—for instance, professional salespeople and political candidates. Then modify what they do to fit your own style. Your image should be a display of your style.

Spend as much as you reasonably can on your clothes, briefcase, appointment book, and pen. People in corporations place a lot of importance on those trappings and may judge your professional abilities by the pen you use. If you have to choose between spending a little more on your image and a little less on computer memory, I recommend going with image. Sizzle sells! If you make a good impression and get contracts, you'll make plenty of money to upgrade that computer later on.

■ **Time to devote to a start-up business.** I'm jealous of teenagers who complain about having nothing to do. Most of us adults don't have that problem. Nevertheless, starting a consulting practice is a lot like buying a house that's a "fixer-upper." You have to put in a lot of "sweat equity." Of course, the more start-up money that you have, the less you'll have to do yourself.

Most of the successful training consultants that I know work at least six days a week, especially when they were building their practices. Rarely do they take "real" vacations, which are never longer than a week. This is part of the price you pay for being your own boss.

For some people, this price is too high. If you value your leisure time, have young children, or are in the infatuation phase of a romance, you may prefer a 9-to-5 job (if one still exists).

Somber personal matters may mean that you don't have enough time available to start a practice. It takes a terrible toll on your time and emotional strength if you, for example, have a child who's undergoing serious medical treatment or if you're caught up in an angry divorce. In cases like these, a switch to consulting probably should wait until the major crisis passes and your time and energy levels are restored.

■ **Ability to accept a little risk.** There's probably never a good time to get married, have children, or start your own business. I believe that the only time you're without worry is when you're dead. We simply can't put off important decisions until everything in our lives is perfectly laid out because that day may never come. No matter how well you plan, nor how smart you are, starting your own business means risk. The question to answer is whether the degree of risk involved is something that you and those important to you can live with.

Before you go hog-wild and quit your day-job, take a moment to review—painfully and honestly—the realities and requirements of starting a consulting business, as well as the personal characteristics you need to become a successful training consultant. Work through the following checklist first by yourself and then with the person from whom you'll need the most support. Your partner's emotional—and possibly financial—support can be a deciding factor in determining whether consulting is the life for you.

Is Consulting the Life for Me? A Self-Assessment

The Harsh Realities	I can live with this	My partner can live with this
1. If you think working for someone else is precarious, try working for yourself.	☐	☐
2. You're not going to get rich quick.	☐	☐
3. Life isn't going to be easy.	☐	☐
4. You'll starve waiting for the phone to ring.	☐	☐
5. Consultants are treated differently.	☐	☐
6. You'll spend up to 50 percent of your time on non-billable work.	☐	☐
7. You'll only get to keep half the money.	☐	☐
8. You'll still have to do work that you don't like.	☐	☐

What It Takes To Be a Successful Consultant:	I have	My partner agrees that I have
9. Money in the bank or an "angel"	☐	☐
10. Adequate insurance coverage	☐	☐
11. A few good friends and contacts or lots of guts	☐	☐
12. Motivation and discipline	☐	☐
13. Strength and survival instincts	☐	☐
14. Presence	☐	☐
15. Time to devote to a start-up business	☐	☐
16. Ability to accept a little risk	☐	☐

Don't expect to have marked all the boxes. If you've marked at least 12 on each go round, you're doing just fine. If you marked fewer than 12, you'll just have to work through this book a little more thoroughly. Good luck!

CHAPTER 2
What's So Great About Consulting?

Many days when I sit at my desk as a consultant, I think, "Life doesn't get much better than this." I can't say every day is a bowl of cherries, but consulting sure does have its advantages. If you play your cards right, you can focus on what you do best and enjoy most, set your own hours, live anywhere you like, and free yourself from office politics and meaningless memos and meetings.

Despite current thinking, I believe that people are not "Jacks of all trades." If you're truly gifted at just one thing, consider yourself fortunate. Becoming a training consultant will allow you to focus on what you do best and enjoy most. That could be developing training courses, delivering training sessions, authoring computer-based training programs, or speaking on a particular topic such as leadership or management development. The choice is yours.

As noted earlier, you'll still have to handle some work that you don't like but as you become established you can spend more and more of your time on the stuff that you do like to do. If you earn enough, you'll be able to hire an assistant or pay temporary help to do some of the chores that you don't enjoy.

Keeping Your Own Hours

Few people work best during Monday through Friday from 9 a.m. to 5 p.m. One of the best things about being a training consultant is having the flexibility to set your own hours. It's easy to work a couple of hours on Saturday morning to make up for the time you spent running a few errands during the week. Heck, you can even take a day off to go fly a plane with a friend or go for a motorcycle ride in the canyons.

Personally, I'm a night owl and work best from 8 p.m. to 2 a.m. That schedule worked great for me when I was a single graduate student, although I admit it hasn't worked as well since I became a family man. But having flexible hours also can be a real schedule-saver for today's two-career couples with children. Shuffling the kids to and from day care, school, and extra-curricular activities is a lot easier if you don't have to punch a time clock.

When you work for yourself, you also have more hours in the day. I once lived in a suburb of Los Angeles, where people spend one to two hours com-

muting on the freeway each day. Most days I worked at home, so I didn't have to be part of the parade of the stalled cars on the freeway. This gave me one to two extra hours of productive time per day that I used to write this book.

Living Where You Choose

Most employees need to live close to where their job is. Consultants have more flexibility. Since you don't have to visit clients every day, you can live farther away from the hustle and hassles of big cities.

Freeing Yourself from Office Politics and Meaningless Memos and Meetings

Office politics and meaningless memos and meetings are what I hated most about the corporate world. Folks such as Peter Drucker and Ron Zemke talk about the time that corporate America wastes doing and producing stuff that's not related to meeting customers' needs: things like hallway conversations, employee-bonding meetings, office policy memos, "pump-you-up" sessions, and birthday parties. I guess these things are important to a certain extent, but another bonus to working for yourself is that you are no longer obligated to be part of them.

Because consultants rarely have to attend events that don't have much meaning for them, they do have to cope with a downside: isolation and not being part of a corporate "family." Bonding with other people and having friends is an important part of the corporate world that you'll miss when you go out on your own.

Some consultants make the mistake of expecting their families to take up the slack. That's too much to ask. Remember that family members can't replace an entire network of people, and they may not enjoy hearing about your work over and over.

Many people cope with isolation by joining a local training professionals' association and making that their professional "home." They also develop a wide network of professional friends and clients with whom they talk regularly on the telephone or meet for lunch. Networking with other consultants and communicating with clients and friends are important parts of being a successful training consultant. They will also provide you with the friendship and human bonding that we all need.

Working Up to Your Potential

When you work for a company, you almost always need to scale back your dreams and draw on less than your full range of talents and skills. The organization's accomplishments have to be more important than your own. As a training consultant, you can finally live and work up to your full potential. Your accomplishments and needs are the ones that really count.

CAUTION: Paying the Price for Freedom

The sticker price for freedom is high, so it's only fair to warn you that there will be times when you work until you feel like dropping. Yes, sometimes freedom requires you to wake at 5:30 a.m. to catch a flight for a client meeting; work a long, full day; then return home at 9:30 p.m. to catch a few hours of sleep before another client meeting being held first thing the next morning. Freedom also regularly requires spending days of non-billable time writing and submitting proposals to present at professional conferences. If any of the proposals are accepted, you'll have the freedom to pay your own travel expenses for the conference. Then there's always the freedom of not knowing when or where your next check is coming from.

So you see that a consultant's life isn't always rosy. But if your strong of heart and pure in spirit, if you're confident about who you are and what you do, and if you're willing to put in the time to learn the survival skills you need to succeed as a training consultant, you're ready to move on to bigger and better things. Interested in getting started? Then let's go.

CHAPTER 3
When Do You Take the Plunge?

Most of the training consultants that I know started without any real plan in mind. The most successful training consulting firm that I know of was started by two friends who were torn between starting their own practice or opening a flower shop. Less than 10 years later, they sold their company for more than 5 million dollars.

I had no detailed plan in mind when I started my own practice. I was Vice-President of Design and Development at a small training consulting firm for just six months when the owner came into my office one Friday to tell me that he couldn't afford to keep me. The following Monday, I started my own firm in a spare room with a cheap telephone, a desk I fashioned out of cinder blocks and a couple of boards, and an extra kitchen chair. From that humble start, I eventually worked myself into a large office with mahogany furniture and hired a private assistant.

But don't be fooled. I was one of the lucky ones. For every success story about a training consultant who went out on his or her own without a plan, there are surely 10 more about those who've failed. Improve the odds that you'll get lucky. Have a plan.

There are three things that separate consultants earning big bucks from those who are struggling to pay their bills: professional networking, speaking, and publishing. I recommend that you start pursuing each of these pretty seriously if you're considering starting your own training consulting firm. I'm not saying that you have to be perfect in each of these areas, but you need to start building your skills so you are at least adequate at all three, darn good at two, and great at one.

Networking

Let's start with networking. As mentioned earlier, your first (and maybe best) clients are likely to come to your attention through people whom you already know:

- people within your own company (in or outside your department)
- training people who work for your company's partners or suppliers

• training consultants or training consulting firms that work with your department.

Of course, you don't want to jeopardize your job by letting these people know that you're preparing to move on, but make sure that they know who you are and the types of things that you do. Create a list of your professional contacts. Keep these people informed of your professional activities and accomplishments. Talk to some of the more influential ones every three months or so.

Being active in professional associations also is a terrific way to expand your contacts and increase your visibility. But being active means a lot more than paying your membership dues and attending annual conferences. It's even more than simply joining a local chapter and going to a couple of meetings. Being active means being involved in the leadership of the organization as an elected officer, as a member of the board of directors, or as a member of a committee. Most national professional associations have local chapters in many major cities in the United States, and some associations have chapters throughout the world.

I recommend working at the local level before you set your sights toward establishing a national reputation. Join and become "active" in at least two professional societies or associations, serve on a couple of committees that you feel you can make worthwhile contributions to, and offer to speak at chapter meetings.

Speaking

In poll after poll, survey respondents cite public speaking as what they fear most (death and fear of flying take turns at second place). But speaking at association meetings and conferences is vital to promoting your training consulting practice.

Most associations are always looking for good speakers for their chapter meetings, as well as their regional and annual conferences. When you've gained some experience speaking at local and regional meetings, target several associations and ask their conference speaker coordinators to send you their Request for Proposal (RFP). They'll be glad to in most cases even if you're not a member.

Because preparing a speech is so time-consuming, be selective about which organizations you wish to speak for. If you're just getting started, you may want to speak to almost anyone who'll listen—just for the experience. As a novice speaker, you'll probably need to be willing to speak for free. At first, you'll even be expected to pay your own travel expenses.

But fairly soon, you'll discover that it pays to be choosy. In most cases, your best prospects for clients will be training directors and human resources managers. These folks are usually members of such professional associations as those listed in the back of this book. Consider yourself lucky if you can get associations to pay your travel expenses and take you to dinner. But when you become a really good speaker, don't be embarrassed to ask to be paid. How will you know when to start asking? Here are a few signs:

- Audiences start to applaud during your presentations, not just when they end.
- Association representatives start to invite you to speak at their meetings.
- Audience members begin to call and write you to say that your speeches have been on their minds and have influenced what they do.

Publishing

Start writing and get published. The newsletter of a professional association's local chapter is a good place to begin. As you get more material published, consider submitting articles to national association journals and business magazines. If time allows, write a book.

Don't expect to make money from having a professional book published. "Then why bother?" you ask. The answer: Do it for the credibility. I have yet to meet a training consultant who wrote a book without having its publicity lead to substantially increased business. A book is marketing magic. Let's hope!

Working It

Everything you do should focus on increasing your visibility in the professional community. I call this working it. Clients develop respect for you when they read an article that you wrote, hear you speak, or learn that you're involved in the management of a professional society. So market yourself as thoroughly as possible by publicizing what you do.

For example, when an article of yours is published in a local chapter's newsletter, send a copy of it to everyone you know or would like to know. You might even send a copy of the article to other professional associations, asking if they would be interested in having you speak during one of their meetings.

Publicize your speaking engagements as well. When you speak at a professional association's meeting or conference, send a copy of the meeting announcement to everyone you know or would like to know. Also send a description of your presentation and any other relevant publicity to the newsletter editors of all the other professional societies to which you belong. Many professional organizations publish notes on the activities of their members. Finally, send your presentation description to other newsletters or publishers of local and national periodicals with a note asking whether they would be interested in an article on the subject.

Remember to include a list of your articles and speaking engagements in your biographical statement.

Putting It All Together

Getting good at networking, speaking, and writing takes time. If you're not the best writer or speaker, try to improve by reading books, taking classes, hiring a consulting coach, or joining an organization like ToastMasters. Even when you're good at it, getting invited to speak, getting your articles published, and being elected an association officer all take time. Most local professional organizations book speakers at least six months in advance, professional publications have approximately a one-year backlog of articles, and it can take three to five years of "active" involvement in a training organization's local chapter before you can become its president.

My grandmother used to say, "Everybody's a specialist." Since you'll spend much time and energy developing your specialties, make sure that they're ones that other people care about, too. I recommend picking a few topics that you feel passionately about and centering your writing, speaking, and committee work on those.

But you also need to make sure that they aren't already addressed by a host of other writers and speakers. Before you try to spread your message to the world, send up a few trial balloons—short articles or speeches—to see whether people express interest or excitement about learning more. You'll soon know whether or not you have a hot topic.

It's also smart to find out who else specializes in your chosen topics. If no one or next to no one is talking about a topic, there's usually a reason. Try to figure out what that reason is. Doing so may steer you away from a topic or may indicate that the topic's just emerging—giving you a chance to establish yourself as an expert in it. If everyone is already talking about a topic, you'll have a hard time standing out from the crowd. Ideally, you want to find a topic that lots of folks are interested in, but only a choice few have begun writing and speaking about.

Taking the Plunge

The beauty in all of this is that when you're finally ready to wave good-bye to your corporate job and join the wild and woolly world of training consulting, you're already there. You're potential clients already know you and respect your expertise. When you start "dialing for dollars," many of the people that you call will recognize your name and be receptive to what you have to say. You may even find that someone sitting next to you at a committee meeting asks whether you know someone who specializes in.... And guess what? This could lead to your first contract.

It's often been said that some people have all the luck. But you know what? The harder you work, the luckier you get.

SECTION 2: HOW TO SET UP AND BUILD YOUR PRACTICE

This section offers advice on how to set up your consulting practice by cost-effectively setting up your office, securing clients, and developing proposals and agreements.

CHAPTER 4
Setting Up Your Office

People will offer you plenty of advice about establishing an office. Most of them will have one hand in your pocket. They'll have attractive pitches for high-priced computer systems, copiers, postage meters, office furniture, and more. Many companies buy lists of new businesses because they know that you are easy prey.

You'll want to buy lots of new things but fight the urge. Far more consultants have failed by running out of cash than by lacking high-rent office space, beautiful furniture, and glossy four-color brochures. Bite your tongue and pinch yourself before you agree to spend a penny. Here's how to set up your office without breaking the bank.

Choosing Where You Work

The worst, most deadly mistake that you can make while setting yourself up as a training consultant is to try to copy the corporate environment that you've just left. There are several reasons why this is a mistake:

✔ You probably can't afford a formal, leased office.

Do you realize how much an "outside" office costs? Do you realize how infrequently clients are likely to visit you? After conducting my consulting activities from my home for a couple of years, my wife wanted me out of the house. I understood her position and, since I was doing well, I leased an office. It was a lovely place that I kept for three years: a two-story Tudor with a breathtaking lobby featuring a magnificent chandelier. My office was in the best location, too—right off the ground floor lobby. In all the time I kept that office, only one client ever came to visit. Most of the time, clients preferred to meet in their offices. The one client who came by was one of my first clients, who had thought enough of my work to give me an $8,000 contract when I was still sitting on a kitchen chair and working on a makeshift desk.

My outside office cost me $600 a month in 1985. Figuring in insurance, utilities, and the premiums that the telephone company and everyone else charges for business service, maintaining that office cost me more than $1,000 a month back then. All that expense to impress one client, who couldn't have cared less where I worked.

✔ You probably don't want a formal, outside office.

The biggest burden of having my outside office wasn't the cost; it was the salespeople who constantly knocked on my door or just walked in to pitch their products and services. People consider an outside office to be public domain, and they'll behave in ways that they never would if they came to your home. Eventually, this got so bothersome that I decided to lock the door to my suite, even when I was there.

Before I took to locking the door, a copier salesperson walked into my suite. I was on the telephone, so I didn't immediately notice he was there. He proceeded to turn all the room lights on and off until I acknowledged his presence. I did, and I told him never to darken my doorway again.

✔ The vast majority of clients don't care (much) about your office.

Many consultants feel guilty about working at home and not telling their clients about it. For business purposes they change their addresses, say from Poesy Lane to Poesy Avenue, and add Suite 100. I used to feel the same way, but I've gotten over it. One day while talking with Daniel, a client with whom I've had a close relationship with for more than 10 years, I unburdened myself and told him that I worked at home. He said, "So what? I've known that for years, and it never made a bit of difference to me."

If you already have clients, I recommend that you check out your assumptions by calling a few of them to ask them how they feel about using firms run from home offices. If they don't care, save yourself some money. If they do care, and they're paying you enough to maintain an outside office, have one. These days, of course, home offices are quite common. Clients who might have reacted negatively five years ago may now see having a home-based business as cost-conscious.

I believe that the fact that you work from home becomes a client's business only if he or she is coming to visit. If a client is coming to your place, say something like this when you're giving directions: "Just so you won't be confused, Poesy Avenue is a residential street. I maintain an office at home, so feel free to dress casually."

What you say isn't as important as how you say it. Practice until you can say that you have a home office without any hesitation or apologetic tone in your voice. If you sound confident, you can turn a potential negative reaction into a positive experience. For example, I had a pool once, and one client who liked to swim always brought a bathing suit to long meetings and swam during lunch.

Some clients may say that they'd like to see your operation before they award you a project. Don't get nervous, just say fine. Few will actually take the time to do so. Besides, if you've been straightforward about the size of your firm, there should be no problem. If they are not yet aware that you run a home-based business, now's the time for them to find out anyway—not after you've spent a week writing a proposal only to find out that they will only work with large companies with expensive offices.

So an outside office is rarely a necessity. What's most important is having a comfortable, quiet place to work. If you can find such a place in your home, great. If you can't, lease an outside office that's functional and cheap.

Outfitting an Office

From the beginning, you'll want and need to create a comfortable and private place to work, but stick to the bare necessities. Of course the specific equipment, materials, and supplies that you'll need depend on the type of training consulting that you'll do. For example, if you're going to publish computer-based training materials, you're going to need more sophisticated computer hardware and software.

My friend Roger Pell says that one should never put money into a depreciating asset. This advice applies to the equipment for your office. Because you're going to need cash for everything from food to postage stamps, I recommend financing your office equipment rather than paying cash. Try to finance through your business bank or wherever you're buying your gear. The office set-up that you should strive for should include the following priority items:

■ The office itself. As mentioned before, you need a quiet place to work, preferably behind a closed door, whether you work at home or lease a space. If you have a house, you might fix up your basement or garage if you lack a spare room. In an apartment, you might set up a folding screen to separate your work space from the rest of the room. Whatever you decide to do, remember that you'll be spending 60 or more hours a week in there. Make it pleasant, business-like, and comfortable. Wallpaper, paint, or a new lamp shade may be all that it takes to make you feel that you're a professional, working out of a professional's office. And a business-like office can help you make the transition from fiddling around with some office work to building a real consulting practice.

■ Storage space. You can't have too much storage space. If you have an outside office, you may have a deep, functional supply closet. If you work at home, you may have to use a standard clothing closet. In most cases, you'll probably need to redesign your closet to give you the largest amount of usable space. Home centers and office supply stores sell racks, shelves, and bins for efficient use of space.

■ Desk and credenza. Functionality and comfort are the most important things in setting up your first office. Since most consultants meet with clients at their locations, any beauty in your office is only for you. Quality chipboard or modest oak probably will be suitable for your office furniture. The purchase of rich mahogany and cherry furniture usually can and should wait.

An "L" or "U"-shaped desk offers the most "real estate" for your money. But I've found that U-shaped desks have lots of wasted space underneath, so I opted for an L-shaped desk with a credenza. This con-figuration may cost a bit more, but it gives you a couple of extra drawers and room for your computer and a few books. Many discount furniture stores offer office sets that include a desk, credenza, bookshelf, and some more goodies. These package deals are often a good buy.

Most people organize their supplies and files poorly. I recommend that you consider the daily, weekly, and monthly technique of office design. It's really easy. Whatever you use daily should be in your desk or credenza. Think of them as high-priced real estate. They should store only things such as pens, paper clips, rubber bands, and your most active files.

Whatever you use weekly should be within easy reach in your storage area, on your bookshelf, or in your file cabinet. Items that could fall into this weekly-use category include less-active files, marketing materials, accounting records, computer manuals, and seldom-used office supplies.

Whatever you use monthly should also be in your closet, but may be stored in a less accessible spot—where you need to move something or use a small stepladder to get to it. Such items as original software, workshop materials, old magazines, and extra binders may be things you want to save for periodic use.

I also recommend following the "one-year rule." If you haven't used something in a year, you probably don't need it and should get rid of it. Many people in the training profession are pack rats. If you're one and can't bear to toss out year-old material, find a space to use as a holding area (e.g., garage) for these items until you're ready to throw them away. Don't let the precious space near your desk become overwhelmed with such outdated materials.

■ Comfortable desk chair. Don't plan to be real productive sitting on a kitchen chair. Even though you may not be able to afford the leather chair that you want, or even a top-of-the-line upholstered chair like the one that you had in your corporate office, you can find a comfortable, ergonomic (that is, back- and neck-saving) chair for less than you might think.

■ Computer system. Choosing your computer system and its peripherals is a major decision, and buying them constitutes a major expense. But you really don't have much choice. If you want to send presentable letters, write decent proposals, and avoid the cost and time lag involved in using outside services, you're going to need an industrial-strength computer and a sturdy laser printer.

I'm not going to go into details of computer speed, random-access memory, or how much disk space you need. Anything that I could tell you would be out of date by the time you finished reading this page! I just recommend that you buy something a bit more powerful than you believe you'll need, and you'll always be happy. I find that I keep a computer about three years and then pass it along to my assistant for another three. I was luckier with my laser printer, which I've had for more than six years. That's because I bought one that was twice as fast and twice as sturdy as I originally needed, and I've loved it every day.

I also recommend investing in hardware or software that lets you back up your files easily. I strongly advise backing up your important files daily and storing them off-site weekly. I once knew a training consultant whose computer was stolen, and she lost six months of work that she'd put into a project. My recommendation is not to let a thief, fire, or your own negligence take away months of your working life. Back-up your files, and store the copies in another building.

■ Telephones, lines, and services. Your first act in starting your own consulting firm should be to install at least one additional telephone line. I recommend that this line ring through only to your office because even if you live alone, you need to separate your business life from your personal life. If you have kids, you probably don't want them to take messages from clients. And if you're lying around in pajamas watching television, chances are that you won't feel like talking with a business associate either.

Most new homes are wired for many telephone lines, but older homes have a limited number of wires coming in from the telephone company. In such a case, if you want more lines, the telephone company needs to run more telephone wire into your home. This takes more effort on the telephone company's part than it normally likes to bother with. But if you're a business customer, they may be more agreeable because they know that you'll make more calls with more lines, which means more money for the telephone company.

The engineers from the telephone company also may try to persuade you to live with what you have. You'll be informed that it's your responsibility to run conduit or build a trench to the end of your property line or something else that sounds intimidating. Getting telephone lines installed is a painful and expensive process that you may as well suffer through only once. My experience is that it's still preferable to do what needs to be done sooner rather than later when it'll start disrupting your business.

Most telephone companies also charge significantly more for business telephone service than they do for residential service. So from a glance at a fee chart, you'd think it would be better to handle calls from a residential line. But most local telephone companies allow business customers to retain their phone numbers in situations that would require residential customers to change them (e.g., after a move across town). And because business customers generate more profit for telephone companies, they get priority service if something breaks down or goes wrong.

There are many telephone services that you can purchase either through the phone company or other providers. Such services include call waiting, call forwarding, and answering services to name a few. Be selective in your choice of options as these features can add up quickly on your monthly bills. Select only the ones that best serve you, your business, and your style. For example, I dislike the disturbance of the not-so-gentle beeping of call waiting, so I don't have it. No matter how well you concentrate or how tactfully you say, "Let's ignore that," your phone conversation has lost its energy and flow. I would rather the caller be routed to voice mail than disturb the conversation I'm already involved in; you on the other hand may feel differently.

I also recommend that you consider having an unpublished or unlisted telephone number. I realize that this may seem like a strange recommendation. But I've found that no one picks a training consulting firm out of the yellow pages, except a tidal wave of telemarketers who want to sell you products and services that you don't need.

Telephones are fairly standard these days. I recommend that you use one with a speaker phone for conference calls, as well as buttons for hold, redial, and speed-call features.

■ Answering machine or service. Some consultants still use answering machines. Others have moved on to voice mail services that many local telephone companies offer. I recently switched to a voice mail service offered by my local telephone company, and it seems to be working out nicely.

A very few consultants use human being-based answering services. This option is only suitable for a handful of training consultants. For example, if you'll have an international practice that involves clients who speak languages other than English and call at times outside traditional U.S. business hours, you may want to use a 24-hour, bilingual or multilingual answering service as a courtesy. Such services are available in larger cities, but they're costly.

■ Facsimile (fax) machine. I bought my first fax machine because I got tired of telling people that I didn't have one, tired of running over to use the one at the local copy shop, and tired of picking up faxes from a service. Once I got my fax, I realized what a wonderful convenience it is. Now I consider my fax machine to be indispensable. It's like a TV with remote control. You don't believe that you need one until you use it, then you can't see how you've lived without it.

Most newer fax machines are equipped with a fax switch that enables your telephone and fax machine to share the same line. This works very well and saves lots of money. In fact, my telephone, fax machine, and modem all share the same line.

There are people, however, who believe that they're taking a moral stand by not purchasing a fax machine. Get real! These days, any training consultant who doesn't have a fax is viewed as a dinosaur.

■ **Bookcases and shelves.** Every consultant needs a couple of shelves to display projects, professional references, and all the erudite books you've read since high school. Any training consultant worth his or her daily rate should be able to fill two floor-to-ceiling bookcases easily. And remember, the quality of the bookcases reflects the quality of the books in them. Not really, but books are heavy so get strong ones.

■ **Filing cabinets.** You'll probably need one or two filing cabinets. For most of us, the ones that hold 8½-by-11-inch paper are fine. But get deep ones. They cost a little more, but they are sturdier and hold more.

■ **Guest chairs.** These are optional. If you're going to have visitors, they'll need something to sit on. Don't worry too much about guest chairs for other consultants or representatives of businesses that you buy from. Wait until one of your clients tells you that he or she is coming to visit before you break out your wallet to pay for an overstuffed chair or two.

■ **Cellular Phone.** For most training consultants, this is optional equipment. If you need and get a cellular phone, look for one that allows you to pre-program a few frequently called numbers and "dial" them by only pressing one button. Also look for one that allows for hands-free talking—and safer driving.

■ **Beeper.** For years I lived in Los Angeles, California, where many folks overestimate their importance. There, even teenagers and homemakers wear beepers. I'm either enlightened enough, or value my privacy enough, not to have one. Because a beeper can be (for now) written off as a business expense, many people who start consulting firms buy one. If you truly need one, get one. But don't believe the saying, "The one with the most toys wins." What do you win if you over-extend yourself in terms of time or money? A nervous breakdown or a spot in the under-employment line.

■ Accessories. You certainly don't need the latest contemporary decor. People expect cutting-edge style from interior decorators, advertising agencies, and art directors. But they expect and want stability from training consultants. Hang modern art on the wall if you like, but don't be too trendy even if you're in future-oriented computer education. Use office accessories that make your office a pleasure to be in: plants, framed degrees and awards, and pictures of people, places, or things that you love. Though you need to be frugal, the money you spend on such items should not be considered frivolous expense. These accessories make the difference between an office that reflects your sense of style, and one that's just a place where you work.

Working at Home—the Disadvantages

My firm is now the size that merits opening an outside office, but I like working from home much better. I'm not evangelical about it, because I know that working from home also has drawbacks. The most difficult obstacles to overcome include the following:

✔ **New consultants never leave their work at the office.**

I don't remember ever meeting a spouse who was happy to have a wife or husband working at home. I believe that one major reason for spousal discontent is that the home-based worker never seems to leave the office. In the corporate world, one goes to work in the morning and leaves at night. At home the office is always open, and the work is always there taunting you to finish it. Don't succumb to the pressure. Instead, establish regular working hours and stick to them.

I had such a problem controlling the urge to wander back into my office in the evenings and on weekends that I actually installed a lock that had to be opened with a key—a key that only my wife had. She opened my office in the morning and closed up shop before dinner. The rest of the time, my little company was closed. A lock might be just the thing you need, too. Maintain your office strictly as a place to work, not the place to retreat to in order to read the evening paper.

✔ **New consultants must balance work/family priorities.**

On the other hand, it may be your roommate, spouse, or child who has trouble staying out of your work space. If you have a spouse or children at home during the day, make it clear that you will keep your office door closed and won't come out to chat or play. Of course, you can agree about the situations that you consider emergencies worthy of being exceptions to your "do not disturb" rule. But generally speaking, keep your office private.

✔ **Many diversions are well within reach—and so is the refrigerator.**

This is a tough one! Working at home gets quiet at times. If you've chosen a room with a good view, you could spend whole days just looking outside watching delivery people and trying to figure out what the neighbors are up to. People who work from home also tend to put a lot of their best toys and equipment in their offices. First and foremost, there's the computer—the biggest black hole for wasted time that ever existed. Other business equipment—for instance, a VCR for reviewing professional tapes—also can lure you away from priority tasks. In some offices, a television, stereo system, camera or, in my case, an electric guitar is not far from reach.

Keeping your office out of bounds for anything but work is crucial to its deductibility. A discussion of the tax situations of the self-employed is beyond the scope of this book. But it's well known that for deductibility the Internal Revenue Service requires that a home office be only an office, absolutely nothing else. If you intend to take a home-office deduction, remove anything that would makes it appear to double as personal space, whether a day bed, a clothing chest, or a microwave oven.

The household refrigerator's also just a short walk away. This isn't a problem if you're not enticed by food. But if you're like me, and haven't missed a meal since high school, you'll need to develop discipline. When I'm working in the office, I usually take lunch about noon and allow myself a piece of fruit at about 3 p.m., when my blood sugar gets low. That's it.

Setting regular working hours also helps you to resist many of the diversions and temptations I've just mentioned. One of the pluses of working for yourself is that you have more control over when you go to work and can organize your schedule to make life more livable and efficient. But you need to get this straight: When you're at work, you're at work; when you're at home, you're at home. And, in Kipling's words, "never the twain shall meet."

✔ **Working at home can get lonely.**

Regardless of what you do, when you work at a company you're rarely alone for long periods of time. You don't do all this socializing when you work at home, so it can get rather lonely and boring at times. In fact, many single people often prefer to work outside the home, so they can meet and interact with other people. Working alone during the day and living alone during the evening provides more privacy than most people enjoy.

Depending on the type of training consulting that you do, you may spend a great deal of time alone, particularly if you're involved in designing and developing training materials. To alleviate your feelings of isolation, try to develop a network of friends to have lunch with. At least make a point of going outside for about a half an hour every day, just to break up the monotony and get some human contact. Pick up a sandwich for lunch or better yet, eat at home then take a walk or ride your bike. But whatever you do, get yourself out of the house.

✔ **Roommates or spouses may not like the idea of you working at home.**

There's a jealousy "thing" that must be overcome if you have a roommate or spouse who works outside the home. We who work at home don't have to put on a suit or pantyhose every morning. I also think that our dear ones suspect that as soon as they hit the road each day, we head for the beach or some other leisure spot.

Roommates and spouses who work in the outside world also deal with many people throughout the day. Once they finally get home, they yearn for a few moments of silence and the time to take off their work clothes. We home-based workers, however, having spent most of the day with no one to share our joys, trials, and tribulations want to talk to some-body—anybody—at the end of the day! For some people, respecting one another's opposing needs can be the most difficult adjustments to make.

Finally, spouses who don't work outside the home immediately lose the privacy that they've cherished. After years of being "out-of-sight, out-of-mind," their home-based better halves now hang around and stick their noses into everyone's business. Guard against this as well. It only diverts your attention from the job at hand and creates animosity within your family.

✔ **A few clients or potential clients may not take a home-based business seriously.**

Some people will only take your business seriously if you have an outside office, an assistant, and a receptionist. I've found this is not the case with training consulting, since most firms are small and clients like the personal service they offer. Still I can't believe how far some small firms go to try to look bigger. They give themselves big names such as the Shocklin Group, which really stands for Henry and Irma Shocklin. Some even get (800) numbers and advertise their national and interna-tional offices, which are really hotel rooms where they may have spent more than one night last year. And many consultants give themselves such fancy titles as CEO, managing partner, or corporate visionary.

I'd bet that you've been thinking about a big name for your firm and a title that would make your company appear to be more than a one-person show. You're wasting your time. Large companies spend mil-lions of dollars trying to look small and personal. You don't need to spend a penny on creating that image; you're already there.

Admittedly I'm sometimes taken aback when a prospective client asks how many people are in my company. But I don't shudder and dread answering the question. These clients already have a good idea of what my response will be. After all, I answer my own telephone. If they'd wanted a multinational firm, they wouldn't have called me in the first place. (I think they ask just to make me feel humble.)

Every once in a while, when asked the size of my firm, I turn the question around and ask the client to tell me what size firm his or her company prefers doing business with. Just about every time I use this strategy, the prospect says that the company prefers doing business with a small firm, because its people can deal directly with management and because they receive a better level of service.

For the few who need a little convincing about using small consulting firms, I stressed the benefits. For starters, clients deal directly with the person or people doing the work. If the consulting firm and client are working together to build and implement a training program, the client gets to talk directly with the project managers and instructional designers and trainers. This may not be the case in a larger firm, where the client typically must talk with an account manager who, in turn, talks to the project manager, who then works things out with the instructional designers and trainers. And as in the childhood game of "Telephone," the more people involved, the more garbled the message becomes at the end.

Besides being clearer, communications and decision making tend to be quicker in a small firm. Often decisions can be made immediately, because the client's already talking to the boss. If a change needs to be communicated or a question has to be answered, there's no problem with calling Accounting. The bookkeeper's right down the hall. There are no interdepartmental rivalries either; there are no departments.

Most clients realize that large training firms usually parade around the generals when they are selling a project, but transfer the project itself to lieutenants and foot soldiers shortly after the contract is signed. Large firms have high overhead. Much of the money these companies bring in goes to advertising, sales expenses, fancy offices, and the generals' salaries. The only way to make money in these instances is to transfer the work quickly to lower-paid foot soldiers. Once these novices become experts, they usually move into management. From there, many move out to start their own training consulting firms. Why not hire the best in the first place?

Of necessity, most large firms also require that their clients fit into their way of doing business. Large firms institute fairly stringent processes and procedures to guide their foot soldiers in getting the job done. Without these rules and regulations, some of the new hires wouldn't know which way to turn.

When clients use small firms, they usually work with the heads of the firm or highly skilled and trusted lieutenants. If small firms use outside resources, they're careful to choose people who are already well skilled, because bringing newcomers up to speed and managing them would take too much time. Small firms also can be flexible about their ways of doing business, because their owner/managers and associates are skilled enough to be able to adapt procedures and invent new methods on the fly.

Finally, even a "good" client is only one of many to a large training consulting firm. And most of the people working on a given project won't be directly affected by the project's success, because the client's money doesn't go directly into their pockets.

Retaining one client and gaining a client's word-of-mouth endorsements may mean life or death for a small training firm or individual training consultant. A single project can mean the difference between a good year and a bad one. One project's success can translate into a new car, another month's worth of paid bills, or even a notebook computer or the children's college tuition. So most small firms focus on delighting their clients every day, in every way possible. So don't be bashful about being a small firm, be proud.

One disadvantage to being a small consulting firm is the lack of back-up help. If you're deathly ill on the day that your client has flown 15 people into town for a workshop, both you and the client are in trouble if the workshop has to be postponed or canceled. So you need a network of professional associates who can fill in when "the show must go on" but you can't.

Throughout this book, I stress the importance of being affiliated with one or two professional organizations at both their local and national levels and networking with your professional colleagues. When you network, consider which professionals might become a back-up system of associates for your firm. It takes time to assess who would do the job in a way that suits you and to build relationships that allow you call on people for emergency help.

CHAPTER 5
Landing Your First Client

Years ago while on a Sunday drive, I noticed a billboard advertising that a company called Wordplex was looking for people to hire. I asked my wife to take down the phone number.

The following Friday I left a brief message describing what I did for Wordplex's Director of Marketing, Ken Walsh, and I asked him to call me back. Then, because it was my day to do errands, I left the office for a few hours. When I returned, I found a message from Ken on my answering machine.

"Boy, what timing!" his voice said. "We were just talking about the need to formalize our sales training program. I'd love to get together with you. Please call me in the office Monday so we can set something up."

I still get goose bumps when I think about that message. I called Ken back right away, but he'd left for the weekend. We spoke on Monday; I gave him a proposal by Friday; and by the following Monday, I had a signed contract and received a check for $8,000. I framed a copy of that check and for many years looked at it whenever I lost heart about finding new clients.

My timing in seeing the Wordplex sign was luck, but making the call was not. Many people whose names I found in similar ways didn't return my calls or told me never to contact them again. But I kept up the effort of seeking contacts and telephoning anyone who might need my services. Perseverance is as fundamental to success as a consultant as technical expertise. You'll need a tough hide carry you through the period when you're looking for your first clients.

Conserving Your Resources

You don't have all year to start earning money. Typically, if a would-be consultant doesn't get a project within 90 days of starting up, he or she is dead in the water.

You can extend the time that you have to look for and land a client, however, if you conserve your resources. To begin with, watch your cash.

Face it. You're going to be facing some financially challenging times. Sure you have to invest in yourself and spend money to make money. But you especially need to allow yourself enough time to find a client. My recommendation is to put a tight clamp on both personal and business expenses. Now is not the right time to trade up to a bigger house or buy a new car. Wait a while.

Meanwhile be good to your angel—the spouse, parent, or well-to-do relative who provides financial, and possibly emotional, support while you're building your practice. He or she deserves some special attention. While you're working on landing your first client, keep your angel informed. If you don't live with your angel, you could call a few times a month to tell what you've been doing. To show your angel that you're out there hustling, you could send copies of articles that you've written or press releases about speeches that you've made. You might invite your angel to dinner once in a while. If your angel is a spouse or significant other, you might offer to do the dishes or take the kids to the park on a Saturday, so he or she can go shopping or play golf. When you do get a client, send your angel a note to say thank you again for the support.

Building on Your Experience

Ironically, I've often found that when someone is really magical at doing something, they'd rather be doing anything else. It's kind of like what "Groucho" Marx said: "I don't care to belong to any club that will accept me as a member."

Let's say that you're the world's greatest sales trainer. Your audiences love you. You carry them to levels of inspiration that others can only dream about. You probably hate being a stand-up trainer and hate working with sales audiences even more. What you really want to be is an instructional designer or a developer of computer-based training, both of which call for skills that you've only developed to a mediocre level.

Please take this advice: When you're starting your training consulting practice, go with what you've got. Build on your successful experience. Be a sales trainer. Put on a few classes. Earn a couple of bucks. Perhaps after you've put more money in the bank, you can move on to designing a few sales training courses. In another year or two, you might move on to develop computer-based training modules on the sales training topics that you know so well. But don't start with a radical move away from your experience. Use your strengths.

Looking for Subcontract Work

It usually takes several months from the day that you first talk with a human resources or training manager or director about a major consulting contract until the day that you're called and asked to submit a proposal. From that point, another year may go by before your bid is accepted and you begin actual, billable work. Consulting is a relationship business, and folks in training tend to be conservative. It's useless—even counterproductive—to try to rush them. So if you plan to keep eating, you need to jump-start your practice while the relationship building necessary for a major contract takes its own time.

If you weren't able to prepare to open your training consulting practice by speaking, publishing, being active in a professional society, and growing a network of professional contacts, you need to find another way to enter the consulting field.

Many new consultants begin by working as subcontractors for other more established training consulting firms. These firms often hire subcontractors to complete parts of projects (e.g., developing a design document or writing a workbook) or an entire project that is part of a larger effort. As a rule, the contracting firm manages the project, maintains most of the client contact, and keeps a healthy share of the fees. As a subcontractor, you may be paid a set price for a specific deliverable or service, or you may be paid an hourly or daily rate.

The good news is that if you're at all connected to the professional training community, it should be fairly easy for you to pick up a subcontract within a month or two of going out on your own. With subcontract work, you usually don't have to worry about getting paid. Most contracting organizations will pay you after an agreed upon period of time (usually 30 days), regardless of when or whether the client pays them.

Finding subcontract work is especially easy if an established training company already has certified you to present its courses. Such companies often receive requests for services that they can't provide using their in-house capabilities, and they're happy to point their clients in the direction of a competent, certified professional.

The bad news about subcontract work is that you'll make less money, get less satisfaction, and won't get to keep the clients. Subcontractors typically earn less than half of what they could earn by working directly with their own clients. Since the contracting organization manages the project and handles most of the client contact, you'll miss most of the fun of working with a client directly and will need to live with someone else's decisions. Finally, the contracting organization "owns" the client, and it's unethical and often illegal for you to try to hustle them. If fact, most contracting organizations will require you to sign an agreement that prohibits you from doing business with their client for at least one year after project completion.

But when you're looking at a pile of monthly bills and a low or negative balance in your checking account, the ability to earn several hundred dollars a day through subcontract work doesn't seem half bad. It will keep creditors at bay and buy you time to sell your services to a client or two of your own.

Selling Your Services

Like most consultants, you probably want to be a salesperson about as much as you want to gargle with sawdust. I was taught that if you learned your craft well, you'd never need to sell your services because people would beat a path to your door. Wrong! Whatever your specialty, there are other consultants who do essentially the same type of work as you. Some do it better; many do it worse; and most potential clients don't know how to tell the difference. If you want to be a successful training consultant, you'd better find some way to let people know you're out there. This is called selling.

Nearly everyone has sold something before, whether it was Girl Scout cookies or even trees in Israel. Most of us didn't particularly enjoy it, but we did it to win a prize or to promote a worthy cause. Selling training consulting services is a lot like that. For many of us, it isn't our favorite pastime, but we know that it's necessary. (I suspect that the consultants who make the really big bucks may even enjoy it a little.)

You've probably done more selling than you imagine. At one time or another, you may have persuaded other people in your company to accept an idea of yours. You may have been involved in convincing other groups within your company to use your department's services. You may even have had a marketing support role, providing technical support to a less technical salesperson. Chances are, you didn't mind these experiences because you were selling what you believed in, not "snake oil." But what do you believe in more than yourself?

To convince prospective clients to use your professional services, avoid any similarity with the telemarketer who disturbed them during last night's dinner. Those well-rehearsed callers sound good for the first 15 seconds, but then you get the feeling that they're slipping their hand into your pocket—and they are. Avoid sounding slick at all costs.

My friend Roger became a very successful salesperson by not delivering slick telephone pitches. He would introduce himself, explain what he did, then say that he'd never spoken with anyone at that company and wondered what they do in the area that related to his work. A few moments of deafening silence would follow, then the person on the other end of the line would pour out loads of information. Roger patiently listened for anything that identified a need that he could meet. You might try this technique yourself.

The major steps to take to sell your services (and products, if you have them) include:

- sending a letter of introduction
- making an initial phone call
- getting permission to stay in touch, or
- scheduling a visit to the client.

✔ Send a letter of introduction.

Probably the toughest part of selling is writing to, or talking with, someone who doesn't know you from a third cousin on his or her grandmother's side. Once you're established, you probably won't have to contact strangers as often. But until you develop a large group of admirers, you'll have be the one to get things started.

Think of how you feel on a day when every stockbroker in the state calls to see if you want an opportunity to get in on the ground floor of some financial venture that you know will be the money loser of the century. The attitude that you develop by day's end is similar to the way that many people feel about receiving "cold calls" (that is, calls that they didn't request).

I recommend sending a letter of introduction to prospective clients before you call them. The goal of a well-crafted letter of introduction is to keep you from being a stranger to the person on the other end of the telephone line. A good introduction letter should spark enough client interest to make a person (at best) receptive to talking with you or (at least) able to recognize your name.

Your introductory letter shouldn't look like a run-of-the-mill sales letter. It must look hand-crafted and personal, or it'll never get past the person's assistant or the trash can. Make it look like a personal note or better yet, an invitation. Make all of your sales communications personal and hand-crafted.

For an introduction letter, I recommend using a good quality note card or Monarch stationery with a bit of a texture. And never use an address label for a letter of introduction. I handwrite my signature on each envelope to show that this is a personalized letter. But don't even think of typing PERSONAL on the envelope. Everyone knows that trick.

Spend time on developing an opening sentence for the letter. Make it a real grabber: If people aren't hooked by the first sentence, your letter will surely end up in a landfill. I've found that the best ideas for hooks come from actively listening to television commercials and studying the junk mail that I bother to open. Some of the slogans that you'll hear or see are legally protected or are too well known to for you to use. But notice how powerful one sentence or question can be? Try to analyze the appeal of slogans that impress you. When you look at mailed marketing letters, you may see words and phrases that you can use or adapt. And, if you've seen advertisements or sales literature from a prospective client, you may work in something that shows your familiarity with the client's business. The following sample letter should give you some ideas for your own.

Sample Letter of Introduction

Mr. Jay Johnson
1433 Davenport Place
Fairfield, New Jersey 07004-2565

Dear Mr. Johnson:

Getting more done in less time—and with fewer people. Is this one of your company's major goals?

My firm can help your training department to do more with less, while avoiding the risks sometimes associated with using an outside resource.

We will accomplish this using a variety of tools and techniques. These include front-end analyses to identify performance gaps; systematic design and development of training programs to ensure thoroughness and efficiency; and ongoing evaluation to ensure curriculum effectiveness.

We also will use the latest media. But even more important, you'll find our methods to be refreshing, innovative, and instructionally sound.

Our experience and expertise in your industry will make us a particularly valuable partner. A five-minute investment of time on both of our parts will tell us whether we can help each other.

Sincerely,

Dr. Joel Gendelman
JG/mh

P.S. I'll call you next week to talk about how we can help each other. If you would like to speak with me sooner, please call me at [phone number].

✔ **Make an initial telephone call.**

I'll give it to you straight: Making these calls is tough. But if you do it well, it can be a most rewarding experience. You'll often gain business and sometimes make new friends.

I used to put off calling "new" people until I heard an anecdote about realtors. Apparently the ones who are most successful enjoy calling people who have listed their homes in the "For Sale by Owner" section of the newspaper. At first this technique sounded about as appetizing as moldy bread to me. But it seems that successful realtors look at it differently. They see these telephone calls as a way of offering help to people who really need it.

I know from experience that selling a home is an arduous and complex process. Many of the people who list homes as For Sale By Owner reach a point at which they realize that they need help. They'd appreciate the services of a competent real estate agent, but they don't know one, or they're too proud to call it quits on trying to sell their home themselves.

The most successful realtors enjoy explaining their expertise to these hardened For Sale By Owner listers. They take pride in helping them to do what they were not able to do on their own—sell their homes—and go on with their dreams.

After hearing this story, I re-evaluated my own attitude toward making cold calls. Instead of looking at these calls as attempts to wangle my way into getting someone to speak with, I began thinking of them as steps in a journey to find people I might be able to help.

I still find that many people have their assistants tell callers that they're in meetings when they're not. A few folks are downright rude. But when I make my weekly sales calls, I always meet someone who's a pleasure to talk with.

Sometimes you won't have the direct-dial telephone number for a prospective client. You're going to need to persuade a gatekeeper to let your call through. Secretaries, administrative assistants, and personal assistants are very important people; treat them like gold. They're often who decides whether you'll get to speak to the person who has the clout and money to hire you.

I've found that the best way to get them to admit you to the castle is to be pleasant. These folks have a tough job and are consistently abused. If you're one of the relatively few people to approach them with respect and a kind word, they'll move the world for you.

When you introduce yourself to assistants, be as formal, or informal, as they are. If the person answers the telephone with, "Hello! Mr. Kellerman's office. This is Tina Shook," introduce yourself by your title and full name. On the other hand, if the assistant says, "Hello! Jim's office. This is Tina," introduce yourself by your first name.

Most assistants will ask you what your call is about. Don't be thrown off balance. They need something brief to say to their bosses or to write on a message slip or e-mail. Be careful to tell nothing but the truth, but don't launch into the whole truth. It wastes time to tell these folks what you really need to tell their bosses. Besides, the more you say, the more likely it is that you'll provide them with an excuse to route your call elsewhere or to say that the company doesn't need what you're selling. Remember that a large part of their jobs is to shield their bosses and get callers off the telephone as quickly as possible. Don't give them an excuse to dispose of your call. If you have sent a letter of introduction, you may simply say, "To continue our discussion." That's not specific, but it will nearly always get you through.

I hate it when salespeople lie to my assistants by telling them that they know me or that the call is a private matter. The moment I realize that the caller is not a long lost friend or relative, I feel deceived. That leaves a bitter taste in my mouth, and I certainly don't want to do business with liars. I do believe that it's OK to say, "Hi! This is Joel. Is Jim in?" But I would never lie if asked whether Jim knows me.

Look for opportunities to make relevant small talk. Secretaries and assistants appreciate a brief conversation that isn't "canned" and acknowledges their work. If you hear laughing in the background, say something like "Boy! It sure sounds like you folks are having a good day." If it's 3 o'clock on a Friday and an assistant says that the boss has left for the weekend, say something collegial like "I wish we had her [or his] hours." Do anything you can to show that you appreciate their role; they'll return the favor.

Initial telephone calls have three goals. First, you need to determine whether prospective clients need what you have to offer and whether they have the ability to pay for it. If so, the second goal is to interest them in what you do and how you do it. Third, you need to convince them that they need to go to another step and let you send them written information or come by for a visit.

Successful initial telephone calls have a structure and sequence. Most telemarketing companies believe that you need to follow a tested word-for-word script to make an effective call. I believe that's only true if you're using contract callers who have little or no knowledge of the product or service that they're promoting. For me, it's a big turn-off if someone calls and sounds as if he or she is reading a script. I immediately hang up.

I believe that you'll do much better with a well thought-out outline of key points. And remember, as with any sales meeting, the objective of these calls is not for you to do all the talking; it's for your prospective clients to share their wishes, hopes, and dreams with you. The following outlines the components of an initial call to a prospective client.

■ Say "hello." A cheery "Hi" or "Good Morning" would be fine, too. Use the prospective client's first name if possible. People love the sound of their own name.

■ Introduce yourself. Tell your name, title, and company. If you have any special designations or ties to the prospective client, mention them. For example, introduce yourself as "Doctor" if you have a doctorate. If you know that you and the other person are members of the same professional society, bring up that connection. If you're active in that professional group (for instance, you're its past president or you spoke at its last conference), mention that as well.

Never mention that you sent a letter of introduction. The person may not have seen the letter or may not remember it. In such cases, mentioning your letter will sound like a challenge and will put the other person on the defensive. That's a sure-fire way to get your conversation off on the wrong foot.

■ "Hook" the prospect's attention. Use a five-second sentence to get the prospective client's attention. This hook should identify a benefit to be gained from using your services or products. It should be similar to the kind that you use in letters of introduction, but worded to be conversational. For example say, "My firm helps companies like yours reduce their training costs."

■ Ask for the prospect's time. This is very important. In the real estate business, agents say that the three most important things about a house are location, location, location. I'm telling you that the three most important aspects of selling are timing, timing, and timing.

If the person that you're trying to talk with is in the middle of a meeting, preparing for a presentation, or almost out the door, now is the wrong time to talk with him or her. Always ask people whether you have caught them at a bad time. If you have, ask them if you may call later and what time of day would be better for them.

■ Provide information about what you can do for the prospect. When your conversation continues, give your prospective clients about 15 seconds of information about how you deliver the benefits that you identified in your hook. For example, if you're selling computer-based training, you might say, "We design and develop training courses that lower your delivery costs, because they don't require the presence of a professional trainer." If you offer team-building workshops, you might say, "We increase the effectiveness of each and every employee by motivating individuals to want to work together and by providing them with clear techniques for doing just that.

■ Ask questions to get the prospective client talking. Remember that the goal of the conversation is to find out whether the person on the other end of the line needs your services, would consider using you as an outside resource, and has the authority and money to hire you. General questions that you might ask include:

* Do you get involved in these areas of training?
* How are you currently handling these needs?
* Is there anything that you're not doing in these areas that you'd like to do?
* Do you use outside training resources?
* Are you looking for ways to enhance your cadre of outside resources?
* What do you look for in an outside resource?
* What do you like most about the outside resources that you're using?
* What don't you like about the outside resources that you've used?

These general questions will, if all goes well, lead to more specific questions related to your services and products.

■ Wrap up the conversation. If it seems that you're barking up the right tree, move to the next step. If the person that you're talking with represents a local company, ask to set up a meeting. If the company is farther away, you may want to send some information first to cement the relationship before you shell out money for an airline ticket.

Before you send information, make sure that the prospective client accepts your invitation to call in a couple of weeks to make sure that the post office did its job and to answer any questions. If the client doesn't agree to accept another call, don't waste the postage or a complete packet of information. You may want to send a form letter that outlines what you offer, but don't hold your breath waiting for the prospect to get back to you.

✔ **Make follow-up telephone calls.**

The most important element in any sales program is to follow up and follow up often. Wait a week or two, then do as you said: Call to make sure that the prospect has received the information and to ask whether he or she has had an opportunity to look through it. If not, ask whether you may call back in a couple of weeks.

If the prospect has reviewed your information, call attention to the client's major needs and point out how you can address them. Next ask, "Does it look as if we may be able to help each other?" If the prospect says "Yes," try to schedule a get-acquainted meeting. If the client says that now is not a good time, ask whether he or she believes that it would be valuable to stay in touch on a quarterly basis.

Always get a client's permission to stay in touch. That way, when you call, you'll be an invited guest, not an intruder.

✔ **Schedule a get-acquainted meeting.**

Inexperienced consultants see a first meeting with a client as an opportunity to sell something. Wrong! Unless you're selling something that costs less than $1,000—and few of us are—the process is more gradual. Look at the first meeting with a prospective client as a means for getting to know each other. It takes pressure off the client and you. Let clients know up front that you view this strictly as an opportunity to become better acquainted. This will make them more receptive to meeting you.

Your goals for this initial meeting are to convince the prospect that you're a credible resource and to learn more about his or her company's need for your services. The rest is detail.

These meetings have a typical format. First the prospect introduces him- or herself and describes the types of work and training the company's does. You introduce yourself and outline the capabilities and experience of your firm. The prospective client talks about his or her wishes, hopes, and dreams for improvements, new ventures, and so on. You talk about how you've helped others to achieve similar wishes, hopes, and dreams. If the expectations that both of you express seem to match, you jointly determine a target date for the next step— which may be for you to come back to meet other company representatives or to submit a short proposal.

The key to success in the first meeting is informality. Avoid hard sell tactics. Approach the meeting as a chance to get to know the potential client as a person, not just a prospective purchaser of your services. Ask when the person joined the company. Depending on how comfortable the person seems to be with your work-related questions, you may ask more about his or her background. People may volunteer information about their hobbies and travels, the books that they read, or their children. This tells you more about how the person thinks and what he or she values.

✔ **Stay in touch.**

As I mentioned earlier, it may take a year or more from the time that you first contact a would-be client to the time when you're asked to bid on a project. Be assured that if you don't stay in touch during that year, someone else will be invited to the party. Staying in touch means the difference between building a growing training consulting practice and fighting for your daily bread.

As a rule of thumb, plan for clients to receive something from you once a month and to hear from you personally no less than once every quarter. That's not as hard as it seems, especially if you use computer software to help you. I recommend Touchbase Pro for MacIntosh computers and ACT for IBM PCs and compatibles.

People take notice when you send them a handwritten note. I recommend that you follow up every telephone conversation with a brief, handwritten note. Try to make it legible, but don't worry about not having copybook-perfect handwriting. Just say that you enjoyed the conversation. Prospective clients will be impressed by the fact that you took time to write. It shows them that you care about building a professional relationship.

Whenever you communicate with a client, keep three phrases in front of you. They're the reasons that people say they choose particular outside resources: I like them; they know my business; they do what they say. If a prospective client thinks this way about you, there's a good chance that you'll be asked to submit a proposal. So move along to Chapter 6 for a discussion of developing proposals.

The Who, What, When, and How of Selling

Before you start making telephone sales calls, you need to have a good idea of the who, what, when, and how of selling. To make sure that you focus your efforts on people who can help you the most, take a minute to read and answer the following questionnaire. Later you may adapt this questionnaire to record information that you learn from sales calls and get-acquainted meetings.

Making Sales Calls: A Checklist

■ **WHO?**

Who have you worked well with in the past? (e.g., human resource executives, manufacturing managers, etc.) _____

_____

_____

Do these people have the need, authority, and money to purchase the products and services that you offer? [] Yes [] No If not, who does?

_____

Can the people whom you're used to talking with recommend you to those people? ☐ Yes ☐ No

■ **WHAT?**

What are the main concerns of the people who recommend or buy your services? (e.g., reducing cycle-time, cutting costs, increasing market share, improving customer service) _____

_____

_____

What major problems are they facing? (e.g., increased regulation, lower profit margins, eroding markets, foreign competition, globalization)

_____

_____

What are their wishes, hopes, and dreams? (e.g., create an impact or secure their own jobs) _____

_____

_____

What do they like? (e.g., security, cutting-edge technology, breakthrough ideas, less involvement, more involvement) _____

_____

_____

Making Sales Calls: A Checklist (continued)

What do they dislike? (e.g., risk or boredom) _____

_____

_____

■ WHEN?

When are your prospective clients likely to purchase the services and products that you provide? (e.g., at the beginning of their fiscal year or at the beginning of each quarter) _____

_____

When are they receptive to considering new outside resources and products? When do they actually make decisions on new purchases? _____

_____

■ HOW?

How do they buy what you are selling?_____

_____

How do they like to interact with outside resources? _____

_____

Do they first like to determine their needs and how to meet them on their own, then consider outside resources? ☐ Yes ☐ No

Or do they get outside resources involved in identifying the need and determining the solution? ☐ Yes ☐ No

Do they have established relationships with other training consultants?
☐ Yes ☐ No

What do they need that they're not currently getting from their established relationships? (e.g., fresh ideas, cutting-edge technologies, dynamic presentations)

_____

_____

CHAPTER 6
Developing Proposals

If you and a potential client have just met and after a little chit-chat, the client asks you to develop a proposal, don't do it. A proposal is a documentation of the sales process, not the sales process itself, and at this point you haven't done any selling. You may not even be sure whether the client is truly in need of a consultant, or whether the company's problem could be solved by merely using a vendor or supplier. You know there are some big differences among the consultant, vendor, and supplier relationships with clients, but the client may use the terms synonymously. Here are some definitions and distinctions among the three terms that you can use to help you clarify the role that prospective clients expect you to assume.

■ Consultant. Consultants are people who are valued for specialized knowledge and expertise in an important or crucial area of business. True consultants usually are called upon when a client has a problem but doesn't know how to solve it. Since the consultant is recognized as an expert in certain topics and processes, the client usually follows the problem/solution process that the consultant identifies. Consultants usually are paid well for their specialized expertise.

When clients and prospects call you a consultant, they're not expecting you to be a "yes-person." They've hired you because of your impartiality and advanced level of knowledge. They expect you to produce the finest of ideas. Since you'll typically be working on strategic issues, clients also expect consultants to learn their businesses and corporate cultures quickly, and to reflect this learning in any solutions that are recommended. When someone calls you a consultant, I recommend that you think of and conduct yourself as if you were a member of their board of directors.

■ Vendor. Vendors are people who sell the service of performing a well-defined task. A vendor usually has some say about how to perform the job, but only within the confines that the client has set up. Vendors usually respond to a Request for Proposal (RFP) that identifies in great detail what the client expects project results to be and the process to follow to get results. Although vendors often are less respected than consultants and enjoy less freedom, they usually are asked to bid on large projects. Clients may not use bidding to hire a training consultant because of the requirement for specialized expertise, but they will put a project out to bid if they intend to use a vendor.

When a client calls you a vendor, you should be aware of a few things. For starters, the client has a good idea of what work they want performed, as well as expectations about how that work should be performed. Several firms are bidding on the project because, despite what the client may say, price will be a big factor in selecting a vendor.

Your response to the Request for Proposal had better describe how you plan to meet the client's requirements. If you believe that some of the requirements can't be addressed or should be changed, you need to have a good reason, and you need to explain it convincingly.

You shouldn't expect special treatment. The client can't give—or even appear to give—any vendor special treatment. If the bucks are big enough, pull in your pride, think about what you'll buy when you're awarded the contract, and submit a proposal.

If you helped the client write the RFP, you have a much better chance of winning. You'll be the only one who can read between the lines of fine print and know what the client really wants. If you didn't help with the current RFP, pledge that if you get the contract, you'll help the client write the next RFP.

■ Supplier. Suppliers are companies that produce commodity products such as nails or pencils. A client seeking a supplier will give several folks the exact specifications of whatever's wanted. The potential suppliers will tell how much they will charge and when they can deliver. Clients consider a supplier's reputation and quality of product, but make no mistake, they are thinking in terms of buying a commodity on the open market and primarily are looking for the best price.

I recommend that you run the other way if a prospective client calls you a supplier. I believe that training consulting is a customized, personal service. Equating consulting with selling an "off-the-shelf" commodity shows a lack of understanding of the profession, and it demeans people who make it their life's work. I'm sure that most people who use the word supplier have no idea of how this term strikes consultants, but its use indicates a mindset that I prefer to avoid.

Preparing To Write a Proposal

There are several activities you must perform before you write a proposal. First, you need to establish rapport with most, if not all, of the people responsible for making the decision to go ahead with the project. Determine their problem, needs, wants, desires, budget, schedule requirements, and other constraints for the project and, based on this information, agree on a general solution to their problem. The next step is to identify the particular benefits your firm will bring to the situation. But before you agree to write a proposal, you need to say something like this to your prospective client:

> "Preparing this proposal will take substantial effort. It will take about two days of my time and more time from my associates. But I'd be happy to write a proposal for you if you're seriously interested in using my firm's services. All that I ask is that when I present our proposal, everyone who has a stake in the project attend a presentation of our ideas. This way we can make sure that we address everyone's needs."

I also recommend trying to find out how many firms will be bidding on a project. It's common for clients to ask for three bids. In fact most companies require three, but I get suspicious if someone is asking for more than four. If I get suspicious, I may bow out of writing a proposal.

In summary, you don't have to write a proposal for everyone who asks for one. A proposal is a sales tool that requires a large investment of your time to develop. You have a right to be selective in determining where you invest your effort.

Submitting a Proposal

If you expect your proposal to do the selling for you, you're in for a surprise. More than likely, a prospective client who asks for a proposal on the first meeting is fishing for free ideas, needs two more quotes to justify using a favored vendor, or requires an internal budget to justify the project and would like for you to draft it for free. *Free* is the operative word here.

Most training consultants develop proposals for free. They want to demonstrate their skills and work with the belief that most clients who ask for proposals will in good faith hire them if they like what their proposal says. But some people abuse the process and want free consulting services gotten under the guise of asking for a proposal. They tell themselves that consultants are rich and that hours wasted on proposals that don't work out are built into consultants' costs of doing business.

If you sense that it's too soon to submit a full-fledged proposal but believe that the request is genuine, I recommend sending a short letter-proposal. If you feel that the client's interest is not genuine, I recommend not writing a proposal at all.

I always put a copyright line (Copyright © [date] by [company]. All Rights Reserved.) on the covers of my proposals. This clearly tells prospective clients that the ideas in the proposal are mine, not theirs. I've never had to call my attorney about this, but I would have no reservations about calling if I found that a client had taken my work and used my ideas without paying for them.

If you get a feeling in the pit of your stomach that tells you that a request for a proposal isn't "real," ask when the client needs to have the project completed. Most people will say "soon" or name a date that's not far off. Reply that your firm is committed to several long term projects and, unfortunately, you won't be able to meet the deadline. Then offer to give them the names of other firms that they could use.

What Makes a Good Proposal

A proposal is a sales piece that summarizes every aspect of your sales effort. It should be upbeat and sales-oriented, but never stereotypically so. Your proposals need to demonstrate to prospective clients that you understand their specific problems, that you know how to solve their problems, and that the clients will enjoy working with you.

A successful proposal has these major sections:

■ Statement of need. This section should include a description of why the client is considering doing the project in the first place. Here is where you need to identify where it hurts. You should make this section clear and concise. It should demonstrate to the client that you've listened well and have a clear understanding of the problem.

■ Business environment. In this section you put the problem into context. You need to identify and describe all the aspects of the client's business that influence the problem: the way the business is organized, the job functions of the people who will be trained, their educational levels, and the factors other than training that may be influencing their performance on the job (e.g., lack of managerial support, faulty or outdated equipment, or poorly designed jobs). You also may describe any influential forces from outside the organization, such as new legislation or competitive challenges, that contribute to the problem or potential for one. This section should demonstrate that you have a good grasp of the environment surrounding the client's problem.

■ Proposed solution. This section is the heart of your proposal: an outline of what you'll do to take away the client's hurt. It needs to be clear, specific, and creative. Include something that the client doesn't expect but that will make a unique contribution to the project. This something extra could be an checklist for managers to use to reinforce the results of the training or it could be an appropriate, creative video scenario. In any case, this section of your proposal should give your client a taste of the excitement that learners will experience as participants in your training program.

But I recommend giving no more than a taste. Many consultants tend to give away the farm. Chances are that your client (or potential client) will be reading several proposals. While it is rare for a client to steal one firm's ideas flagrantly and select a firm that submits a cheaper price, it does happen.

■ "Our" approach. Now that you've made promises to the client, you have to prove that you have a plan for making good on them. In this section, you lay out exactly how you're going to move the client's organization from where it is now to where it wants to be. Include just enough detail to prove that you know what you're doing and how to do it.

Again, avoid including so much detail that the client organization has a blueprint for doing the project itself or taking your well-thought out plans and professional secrets to a lower bidder. All you really need to do is provide enough detail to convince your prospective client that you have the expertise to deliver what you promised. If for some reason, the client asks for more detail than you believe is necessary, be wary.

■ Benefits of our proposed solution and approach. This section should, in a straightforward way, tell the client why your solution and approach are the best by identifying the specific benefits that the company will enjoy as a result of hiring you. These benefits should relate to the real world by being practical and substantial. You need to spell out how choosing your firm will help the client make more money, spend less money, increase market share, enhance customer service, or react faster to changes in the marketplace.

Notice that we haven't gotten to the price yet. There won't be a section called "Price" or "Investment." Price often is the first section that clients look for, but don't give it until you convince them that your ideas are worth the few extra dollars that you may be charging. Most clients prefer a process that ensures success, requires a minimal investment of their time, reflects the culture of their organization, and will be flexible enough to adapt to their changing needs. Show how your process will suit those preferences, and you'll get the company's business.

■ Project specifics. Here's the section that makes the purchasing people, finance people, and other analytical people happy. This is where you'll tell them exactly what they are getting in terms that can be counted. These include, but are not limited to the

- number of pages in instructor guides and participant manuals
- number of audio, video, and computer-based training (CBT) minutes
- number of screens of CBT information
- format of master materials
- number of workshop days
- number of times each workshop will be conducted
- number of scheduled hours for set-up, instruction, and follow-up activities
- price.

Note that the steps in the process that you've proposed are interrelated and are to be taken together. Many prospective clients ask for an à la carte menu approach that allows them to bypass certain services or skip products that you propose. The menu approach is fine for ordering dinner because each item is prepared separately, but it doesn't work for

developing programs where each deliverable and step in a process usually is contingent upon the others. If, for example, Step 3 is predicated
upon information gathered in Step 2, and a client only wants to choose
Steps 1 and 3, you'll wind up doing Step 2 anyway. You just won't get
paid for it.

   If you believe that a small shift in sequencing is feasible, you may
agree to it (although you're setting a precedent that may come back to
haunt you). But if the shift undercuts any chance of success or the prof-
itability of the project, stand by your original recommendation.

■ "Our" experience. Many, probably most, clients don't usually read
past the price. But in case they do, you should describe the experience
of your firm to assure them, beyond a shadow of doubt, that you have
the power to deliver the goods. Include descriptions of similar projects
that you've performed for companies in the same, or similar, industry.
Summarize your firm's other experience to show how your vast expertise
equips you to deliver the benefits of the approach that you identified
earlier in the proposal.

■ Project personnel. This section will look like a series of summarized
resumes, but it's more than that. Remember, a proposal is a selling document and its every word should focus on convincing the client that your
firm is the only one qualified to do the job. In this section, describe the
pertinent skills, education, and experience of the people who would
work on the project. Make their professional biographies sound as if
these people were born to get together to do this particular job. I recommend that you not include the last names of the people that you recommend. The training world is small, and lots of stealing of associates
and staff goes on.

■ Final word. This is where you appeal to the client as a person. This is
the section to spend the most time on. It should not leave a dry eye in
the house. I can't tell you what to say. You need to say the right thing in
just the right way. You can only find it by thoroughly understanding the
essence of what the client wants from your relationship. It should reinforce your personal commitment to the project, and it should be hand-
signed.

   If at all possible, your proposal should be presented, not mailed or sent by a delivery service. Your presentation should be organized to correspond with the sections of your written proposal. Highlight the key points, always remembering that you're selling a group of business people on using your services. Training managers and executives rarely make rash or emotional decisions. Most of them are skeptical of salespeople and nearly all of them are turned off by "hype." I recommend playing it straight, being professionally friendly, and giving them the information that they need to select your firm.

Remember that you need to sell each and every person involved in the project before you ever write a proposal. Nothing new should be happening at this point. All your great ideas and benefits should have been presented to each person and approved, individually, during the sales cycle. A good sales cycle is a series of small steps that leads you to winning the project. If you've received approval from all interested parties all along the line, you have nothing to worry about.

Your proposal presentation is an opportunity for everyone to get together and feel good about the project—good enough to say OK, let's run with it.

If you feel that everything is riding on this one meeting, you're already in trouble. The objective isn't for you to say as many flowery words as you can. It's to make everyone comfortable enough with the project to want to spend money on it. I recommend that you make your presentation less of a presentation, and more of an interactive discussion. Get them to talk. Ask them if this makes sense to them. Ask whether they see the benefits. Ask whether they believe that you're all moving in the same direction. Ask if this feels right to them. Use words and phrases that address all of the clients' senses; their senses of sight, touch, hearing, taste, and smell.

You may use overhead transparencies, slides, a computer, or just a sight-seller to make your presentation. You'll need to do what your client expects and keep pace with the competition, but in a homespun way. A homespun touch is important and in keeping with the personalized nature of small firms. Use high-tech presentation devices as necessary, but add a high-touch extra. I know of one training consultant who always brings fresh-baked cookies to proposal presentations. What a great idea! I wish I'd thought of it.

CHAPTER 7
Setting Up the Business
Aspects of Your Practice

For many people, setting up the business aspects of a training consulting practice is a painful step that they avoid until it becomes unavoidable. For other people, it's the step that they perseverate on for months because they're deathly afraid of getting down to real work. My priorities for running a training consulting practice are simple:

- Sell my services and products.
- Perform the services and produce the products.
- Get paid for my work.
- Take care of all the rest.

To me, setting up the business aspects of a practice is part of "all the rest." But if you haven't gotten around to addressing this process within the first six months of starting your practice, you really should get started.

Setting Up as a Small Business
To set up your practice as a small business, you'll need to do the following:

✔ **Open a separate business checking account.**
For accounting purposes, you need to separate your business finances from your personal finances. Your first step is to establish a separate business checking account from which to pay your business expenses and in which to store business income. Never, never, I mean never, put business income into your personal bank account or write checks to cover business expenses out of your personal checking account. Doing so will double the time that you spend accounting, really upset your accountant, and leave you wide open for an audit.

In the beginning you'll have more expenses than income, so open your business account with a loan from yourself written on your personal checking account and posted to "Loan from Owner." Don't wait until you've chosen a business name to start a business checking account. It may take time to choose the name that's just right for you. Meanwhile you can be setting up your office. Once you decide on a business name, simply close this account and open one in your new business name.

✔ Develop a relationship with a bank.

Your banker is one of the most important people in your business life. He or she can make sure that you don't have to wait weeks for your client's checks to clear. Your banker also can make it much easier and somewhat less expensive to buy or lease a car and other necessary business equipment.

I recommend banking at a local savings and loan. They tend to be smaller, have a more personal atmosphere, and cater to small businesses. Most training consulting firms, like other small businesses, don't need the big-business services of a large bank, but they do need personal attention and the comfort of seeing a friendly face.

Look for two important features when you choose a bank. First, you'll want a bank that doesn't put "holds" on checks from major corporations. When you finally get a $35,000 check that you've been waiting 60 days to receive, you certainly don't want to wait another 14 days or more for it to clear. I have arranged with my banker to have any check from a major corporation treated as cash as soon as I deposit it.

Second, you'll need a small line of credit or overdraft protection. If you're spending your time selling business and making business, you occasionally are too busy to realize that you are a couple of hundred dollars down in your business checking account. Try to arrange for a few thousand dollars leeway to cover your frantic weeks, bad memory, and the 60-day lull before that $35,000 check shows up. At the time that I wrote this book, a line of credit for a small business was hard to come by. For this reason, I keep a couple of credit cards—the banker of last resort—with several thousand-dollar credit limits to carry me through tough times. The cards may have annual fees, but if you don't let your debt grow, you get a grace period that will give you great piece of mind.

The best way to develop a relationship with your banker is to see him or her frequently. I recommend that instead of sending your assistant to the bank, you stop by yourself. Be sure to say "hello" to the branch manager and mention how well you're doing.

✔ **Incorporate or establish a DBA (Doing Business As).**

Once you've chosen a name for your practice, you need to do one of two things: Create a separate business entity (that is, incorporate) or establish yourself as someone who is doing business under a different, company name. People used to think that all businesses need to be incorporated, but that's not true. There are advantages to incorporating, particularly with regard to avoiding personal losses to cover the liabilities of your training consulting practice.

However, this limited liability comes at substantial cost. It costs a good deal to set up and maintain a corporation. Many books claim that they'll help you incorporate without an attorney, but it's a risky choice. You'll probably need an attorney to set up a corporation and an accountant to keep it going.

Corporations must meet much more stringent financial-reporting requirements than individuals do. You'll need to file a separate annual corporate return, as well as quarterly returns. While most consultants acting as sole proprietors can take care of their own accounting, you'll probably need an accountant to handle your accounting if you incorporate. These services will add several thousand dollars of expenses to your balance sheet at a time when you're not making much money.

The important benefit of a corporation is that you are not liable for its mistakes. If you expect to received a large loan from a bank, have many employees, or deal with hazard and safety issues (e.g., if you provide safety training to operators of nuclear power plants), a corporation is what you want to be.

To learn more about setting up a corporation, I recommend that you ask other training consultants who have incorporated to refer you to the attorneys who handled it for them.

Another way to set up your company is to establish that you'll be "doing business as" (DBA) whatever your firm's name is. You'll need to do this before you can open your "real" business account.

Just call your local newspaper to ask how much a DBA costs. Most newspapers run such notices. The smallest newspapers have the cheapest rates, so try these first. (Frankly, no one cares whether your DBA was listed in *The Wall Street Journal* or your hometown gazette.) When you pay for a DBA announcement, a newspaper prints a notice for a couple of weeks stating that you intend to use a certain name for your business and that if anyone objects to it, they should speak now or forever hold their peace.

A DBA is not a trademark. It offers very limited protection. If you're seriously concerned about protecting your firm's name, consult an attorney who specializes in this area.

✔ Obtain a business license and a resale permit.

Depending on where you live, you may need to get a license to do business. As a rule, this isn't very complicated. The most difficult part is paying the couple hundred dollars a year that the local jurisdiction can tax your firm. Some people say that you can get away without it, but I don't recommend breaking the law—it's not worth the risk. Just call the city or county clerk, send in the paperwork and money, and be done with it.

States can only receive tax on an item once. Let's say that you buy 100 binders to use for training courses. Your local office supplies store charges you tax, so the government has made money once. When you sell those training courses to your clients, you charge tax. Then the government has made money twice. But the government is only able to tax an item once; hence the concept of a resale license.

When you buy the binders, tell the store that you have a resale license, and the store won't charge you tax. But when you sell your courses, you charge your customers' tax, and then send the state its fair share. Now the government only makes money once, and "all's right with the world."

Why doesn't every training consultant have a resale license? Most training consultants don't believe that what they sell is a tangible product, like a coat or a car. They believe that they sell a service, comparable to time spent with a doctor, lawyer, or dentist who analyzes a problem and offers a solution. States don't charge sales tax for services, only products.

Do you need to get a resale license? As a training consultant, you need to get a resale license when you begin selling products. I define *product* as anything that will look and feel (literally, is tangible) like a finished product to clients. For example, a draft of a new employee orientation course may not be a "finished" product. But say the client has you print, bind, and deliver 1,000 copies. That sure sounds like a product to me.

To avoid paying tax on printing and binding, you need to have a resale number. To avoid going to jail, you'll need to charge your customer tax on the printing and binding portion of the project, and send that tax to the state on a quarterly basis. To receive a reseller's permit, call your State Board of Equalization. It's listed under the State Government in your local telephone book. If you're not sure whether you should charge a client a sales tax, you probably should. I have a paragraph about sales taxes in my agreements with my clients. This paragraph specifies that if the state comes after me for back sales taxes, I can come back to my client for them. If you're still confused about the whole issue of what is taxable and what is nontaxable, join the club. When deeply in doubt, consult a good accountant or tax attorney.

✔ Develop relationships with an accountant and an attorney.

Although other relationships may be more fun, there will come a time when you need one of these professionals to look out for your interests. I've always found that the best way to choose any type of professional is to ask other training consultants whom they use and have been happy with. Pick someone who works with professionals and consultants; someone who seems knowledgeable and credible; and especially, someone whom you trust and get along with. You'll be working with these people during emotional times, and dealing with someone you like will remove one more problem that you don't need.

✔ Develop standard agreements.

Crafting agreements with your clients—and with your outside resources—is discussed in the next chapter. At this point, suffice it to say that you should never do anything without an explicit written agreement. Every time I have, regardless of how comfortable I was with the person I was doing business with, I always got burned.

✔ Develop invoicing and accounting systems.

When they're making money hand over fist, some consultants ignore cash flow. Only when things slow down a bit do they look into their files of outstanding invoices to see who owes what. The key to managing your firm's money effectively is to get it in hand as soon possible and then hold on to it as long as you can.

Independent training consultants often have trouble managing cash flow. They're too busy selling their work and doing it to worry about whether they're getting paid for it. I know some consultants who take a month to get an invoice out. Letting invoices go unpaid isn't smart even if you're rich. Training consulting is like any other business. To stay in business you have to be on the plus side of the ledger sheet most, if not all, of the time. To keep on the plus side, remember to:

■ Get partial payment up front. No lawyer would consider taking a case without a retainer, and neither should you. Ask for at least 20 percent of the cost of the project up front. This will ensure that the client is committed to the project and that you're paid for the work that you are about to do.

■ Invoice as soon as possible, and ask for payment within 30 days or less. No individual and no business likes to wait for money—not even the elite Fortune 500—but least of all consultants and the people who work for them. Small firms such as yours can't afford to wait. As a rule, wait 30 days at most. If for some reason a client won't agree to pay within 30 days of receiving an invoice, insist on a larger retainer.

Invoice clients as soon as you have completed a service that you can bill for. If you are to be paid after you deliver a design document, deliver the invoice with the document. If you're to be paid after you present a workshop, bring an invoice to the workshop. Better yet, send the invoice a couple of weeks in advance and arrange to be paid the day of the workshop.

■ Do semi-monthly or monthly accounting. If you're like me, tackling money matters once every two weeks is about all the accounting you'll be able to take. I use the shoe box method. All bills go into a shoe box (you may use a file) to be sorted out and paid later. At first I paid bills once every two weeks. Recently I switched to paying bills once a month, but I still write a few checks mid-month for the bills that would otherwise incur interest or finance charges.

There are many good computer accounting applications that can help you manage your bookkeeping. But don't ask your accountant for a recommendation. Your accountant probably would recommend the full-featured and difficult to use application that he or she uses. That kind of software makes an accountant's job easier but your job a lot harder. Instead, ask your professional friends to tell you what they've found to be easy to use and moderately priced.

■ Follow up on invoices. Don't expect clients to pay you on time automatically. Left to their own devices, most accounting departments would wait 90 days or more to pay you. Not a pretty picture.

Put copies of invoices into a box or file that you check every couple of weeks, or make notations on your calendar indicating who is supposed to pay you, for what, and when. If payment hasn't arrived within a couple of days of when it was supposed to, call your client.

If the client prefers, agree to call the accounting department once. But don't take over the client's responsibility to make sure that you get paid.

It's better to have someone else call to ask clients for payment. Your relationship with a client is less likely to be impaired if someone else is the bearer of unpleasant news, so have your assistant call if you have one. Whether your assistant calls or you do it yourself, take a polite approach. If you've done a good job, most people will want to see that you get paid and stay in business.

When you call to follow up on an invoice, the client will know that you are serious about getting paid on time. Because the client won't want to be bothered again, he or she will probably send a clear message to the accounting department to make sure to pay promptly.

■ Pay yourself first. If others have been involved in the project, your first inclination is to pay them as soon as you get paid. Just as you expect and appreciate being paid promptly, so will they. Paying your resources promptly is the best way to ensure that they'll continue to do good work for you. But never take the money out of your own pocket! I recommend that your agreements with outsider resources state that they'll be paid within 15 days of the date that you're paid. If you can, pay them sooner; they'll appreciate it. But never pay them with your own dollars.

Staying Ahead of the Game

Earlier I mentioned the importance of billing a client after each project milestone. But how much should you bill your client per milestone?

Follow these guidelines for scheduling your payments:

- Get as much money as quickly as possible.
- Tie each payment amount to the client's perceived value of each milestone.

• Schedule payments to make sure that you have been paid for your time and expenses in advance. This way, no matter what happens to their project, you'll be paid for your work.

I'm not advocating that you should arrange payment so that you get paid for work you didn't legitimately perform. Projects will change, slow down, or stop for a variety of reasons. Many of these reasons will have nothing to do with you. I'm only advocating making sure that you can afford to be flexible in face of the winds of change, because you're assured that you'll be paid for your efforts.

All of this establishing and organizing may seem overwhelming, particularly if you try to do it all at once. Keep your priorities straight. If you wait until all the business aspects of your practice are in order before you get on the phone and start hustling for business, you'll soon be out of business. Cover the basics, then do the rest as needs arise: Develop a standard contract when you get your first client; open your "business name" checking account when you get your first check, and so on. Keep in mind that as long as you're making money, the rest is detail.

CHAPTER 8
Putting It in Writing:
Developing Fair Agreements

You can't be sure of many things in this world, but there's one thing you can bet on. If you do business without a written agreement, and I don't care whether it's with your best friend or your grandmother, it will turn out to be a tragedy for both of you. Just like children, adults get along best when they have limits and guidelines. Write this somewhere where you'll see it and remember it:

Never do business without a written agreement.

But what if you've done business with the client dozens of times and good old Ed says that the signed agreement is in the mail? Fax the client a short agreement that ensures that you'll be paid an hourly fee for any work performed should something happen and the deal falls through before the original agreement is signed and sealed. Have the client sign and send back this short version. With all the reorganizations, mergers, and bankruptcies in the world today, you just can't be too careful.

The goal of a well-written agreement is to ensure that everyone understands and agrees about what they're supposed to do. That's why I call the document that I ask my clients to sign an *agreement* instead of a *contract*. Contracts are long scary documents in which someone tries to put something over on you. Contracts are something that you need to send to your legal department. Agreements are more like letters between friends. A well-written agreement should be a simply-written document that clarifies your relationship with a client or an external resource.

Most training consultants bill for their services in one of two ways: for a fixed price or for time and materials. Let's look at what each type of agreement should include, starting with the fixed price. For the purpose of the examples presented, FT refers to the consultant and FCA refers to the client company.

Drafting a Fixed-Price Agreement

Under a fixed-price agreement, you charge a set fee for a project. Some training consultants include everything in this one price. Others may bill travel, shipping, and telephone expenses separately. The advantages of working with clients under a fixed-price agreement are that you usually get more money up front, clients seem to like it better, and you don't have to do much record keeping. The big disadvantage is that you assume a great deal of risk. A fixed-price agreement with a client should include these essential sections:

■ Scope of work. Clearly describe what the client is to get for the money paid. State the goal(s) of the training program and describe its physical deliverables. These descriptions of the deliverables may include

- estimated length of the course
- number of pages or audio/video/CBT minutes of instruction
- number of training modules or sections
- number and quality of illustrations
- format(s) (e.g., electronic files or audio/video masters).

Example: Design, develop, and produce self-paced training course to train employees to enter information and analyze reports produced by, or within, TRACKS. This course will have three separate parts and take up to five hours for participants to complete.

Materials for this course will include
• a tutorial and mastery test of up to 120, 8.5-by-6.75-inch pages
• 15 simple illustrations or flow charts
• a data diskette with sample data.

■ Security interest. A statement indicating that you own the work until the client pays you in full.

Example: FT retains a security interest in all such items until the purchase price has been paid in full.

■ Payment. Identify how you'll be paid. Training consultants working on a fixed-price contract typically are paid for each project milestone that they complete. Include a start-up payment because accomplishment of the first milestone may be weeks away, and additional milestone deadlines may be months away.

Example: FT will be paid $100,000 according to the following payment schedule:

Project Milestone	Percentage
Project start up	25%
Delivery of design	15%
Approval of design	15%
Delivery of drafts	15%
Approval of drafts	15%
Delivery of produced masters	15%

■ Termination. Identify what happens if you or the client chooses to terminate an agreement, or if either of you wishes to reschedule the performance of your services. The key is to be as flexible for the client as you can, while still being fair to yourself.

Example: Either party may cancel this agreement with two weeks written notice. If FT cancels the agreement, it must provide FCA with copies of materials corresponding to all project milestones that FCA has paid for.

If FCA cancels this agreement, FCA must pay for all milestones completed and approved, as well as for any additional work completed on a time-and-materials basis according to FT's standard billing rates.

If FCA cancels this workshop within one week of the implementation date, FCA and FT may reschedule the workshop to a mutually convenient date. If FCA provides less than one week's notice, FCA is responsible for payment in full.

■ Project review points. Revisions are a problem in every project. Clients want the ability to make revisions until a project's very end, but would rather not pay for this flexibility. If you have the luxury of bidding a project high enough to include a 10 or 20 percent revision factor, you'll be fine. But these days, building in a revision factor may price you out of the competition.

To minimize the number of revisions, have the client authorize one person up front to make the final decisions on each step in the project—and make that person honor his or her decisions. This section of the agreement is an identification of the decision-maker and his or her responsibilities.

None of us is perfect, so I recommend quietly making an extra, but useful, change or two if these arise after a milestone has been approved. But don't let matters get out of hand. At some point, your client needs to know that changes take time and that you must be paid for your time. I have always found that communicating this from the beginning convinces clients to take their reviews seriously and to carefully assess the importance of changes they might wish to make after a milestone has been approved.

> **Example:** FCA shall expeditiously review material submitted at each review point by FT. Any costs associated with FCA changes subsequent to FCA written approval of a particular review point shall be borne by FCA.

■ Sales-and-use taxes. At the time this book was written, state governments didn't require businesses to charge tax on their services, but did require them to collect taxes on goods. Most consultants view their work as providing a professional service. At some point, however, a state may disagree with you about this. You need to make sure that if this happens, you'll be able to go to your client for the taxes owed and not have to pay them out of your own pocket.

> **Example:** FCA shall be responsible for and will pay all applicable sales-and-use taxes directly to FT. FCA also will pay any additional taxes upon submission of a bill from appropriate tax authorities.

■ Client/support activities. Peter Block's book, *Flawless Consulting*[2], stresses the importance of being authentic in dealings with your client. The most important area of honesty is that you and the client are a team. Regardless of how good you are at what you do, you can't succeed without client involvement. This section is an outline of the resources and activities that your client needs to provide in order for the project to succeed. These resources and activities may include, but are not limited to the following:

- a project manager or client representative who has authority to approve project milestones and the responsibility to act as the focal point for the client's efforts
- other people (e.g., experts to interview, training representatives who participate in preview/pilot testing of a course, four to eight trainees who meet the course requirements to test the training program)
- equipment, facilities, and people (e.g., subject matter experts, any equipment needed to complete training)
- information (e.g., product brochures, manuals)
- people, equipment, and facilities that are needed to test and implement the course
- thorough, timely review of each stage of your work
- performance of each activity according to a mutually agreed upon schedule.

> **Example:** FCA will be responsible for:
> - assigning a project manager who will be responsible for coordinating and approving all aspects of each stage of the project
> - providing subject-matter experts and representatives of the target audiences as required for information gathering, review, and testing
> - providing four to eight people who meet the course entry requirements to test the training program
> - providing reasonable and timely access to all facilities, equipment, and people for purposes of research, review, and program testing
> - providing correct and timely information to include in course outlines and manuals relevant to the program's subject matter
> - reviewing materials in a timely manner
> - adhering to the schedule identified in the proposal or any mutually agreed upon revised schedule with respect to reviewing and approving review points, completing major milestones, and finalizing product development.

■ Reimbursed expenses. The trend is to bundle all travel, lodging, and incidental expenses into the price of larger projects. For a smaller project or projects for which you're competing strictly on the basis of price, you may want to bill expenses separately. Typical expenses include travel, shipping, copying, and telephone costs.

> **Example:** FCA shall reimburse FT for the following expenses in connection with this project:
> - travel expenses, including air fare, local transportation, lodging, and meals
> - telephone expenditures
> - postage, copying, and freight/shipping expenses

■ Delays. Unexpected things happen—some of which wreck schedules. But you shouldn't be responsible for making up the difference if you weren't the cause of the delay. This section is a statement that you cannot be responsible for delays caused by your client or acts of nature.

> **Example:** FT shall not be liable for delays caused by FCA. Neither FT nor FCA shall be liable for delays in delivery or failure to produce due to acts of nature including, but not limited to, fires, floods, earthquakes, strikes, or civil disturbances.

■ Demonstration copies. You can't imagine how hard it can be is to get copies of your work, especially if your client is responsible for reproducing it. After a project is over, people get wrapped up in other things. But a major factor in prospective clients' choice of training consulting firms is their reaction to samples of similar work the consultant has done for other companies. One of your greatest assets as a training consulting firm will be copies of the work that you've done for your clients. This is a client's acknowledgement of an obligation to provide you with those samples.

> **Example:** FT shall be provided with two (2) complete reproduced copies of all deliverables under this agreement.

■ Right to use copies. Having samples of your prior work isn't the same as having a right to use them. This section is a confirmation of the client's permission for you to use samples in sales calls and presentations.

From time to time you'll get involved in projects that contain material that could be of interest to a general audience (e.g., teamwork, territory management, sexual harassment). Developing off-the-shelf products should be a goal of every training consultant. But how do you come up with these products? You can't invent them from air. You get them by putting together bits and pieces of the work that you've done for others. This section also may be used to raise the issue of your being allowed to take nonconfidential bits of your work for the client and mix it up with pieces of work that you've done for others to make a new product that you may resell.

> **Example:** FT shall be allowed to use nonconfidential portions of demonstration copies for internal applications, capabilities demonstrations, and sales promotion purposes upon written approval by FCA.

■ Confidentiality. Most clients expect confidentiality. Instead of making them ask for it, include it as part of your standard agreement. Clients will respect this reflection of your professional integrity.

> **Example:** FT agrees that the subject matter of the services provided to FCA shall be confidential and, therefore, FT will not disclose such information to any third party.

■ Arbitration. Major corporations have the legal staffs and money to keep you in court for life or at lease until your training consulting firm goes bankrupt, whichever comes first. Including an arbitration clause ensures that you have a cost-effective means of resolving your differences should problems occur.

> **Example:** Any dispute or controversy arising under or in connection with this agreement shall be settled exclusively by arbitration in [city, state] in accordance with the rules of the American Arbitration Association in effect at the time. Judgment may be entered on the arbitrator's award in any court having jurisdiction. All costs for such arbitration, as well as any attorney fees and costs incurred in enforcing this agreement, will be paid by the prevailing party.

■ Project schedule. As anyone who's gone through home renovation can tell you, a project without a schedule tends to go on forever. Include a schedule that, more often than not, is the timetable that your client already has asked for and that you have agreed to. If necessary, you and the client may decide to change it later, but it still helps to have something to work from.

Example: The following tentative timetable has been agreed to by FCA and FT:

Activity	Dates
FT gathers information	4/20–4/25
(interviews)	4/23–4/25
FT creates design document	4/26–5/5
FCA reviews design document	5/6–5/10
FCA/FT review design document	5/11
FT revises design document	5/12
FCA approves design document	5/13
FT develops drafts	5/14–6/10
FCA reviews drafts	6/11–6/16
FCA approves drafts with modifications	6/17
FT revises drafts	6/18–6/25
FCA/FT Pilot test	6/26
FT produces camera-ready materials	6/29–7/13

Two samples of fixed-price agreements appear in the appendix in the back of this book. One covers a training course development project, and the other covers implementation of a workshop.

Drafting a Time-and-Materials Agreement

Many professionals—especially lawyers and accountants—don't work for a fixed price, but do business according to time-and-materials agreements. Under this type of agreement, you charge a client a set fee per hour and a set percentage of mark up on all outside purchases. The advantage of using this type of agreement is that you assume no risk. The disadvantages are that clients are skeptical of it, you have to do more record keeping, it may breed mistrust, and it means that you get don't get much money up front. And most clients insist on a "not-to-exceed" estimate (a ceiling figure) to supplement a time-and-materials agreement. When you set a ceiling figure, you lose the advantages of a time-and-materials agreement, but retain all the disadvantages. In such a case, you may as well bid a fixed price for a project.

An agreement for a project done on a time-and-materials basis is simpler than a fixed-price agreement. Such an agreement typically includes these sections:

- Scope of work
- Payment
- Client-support activities
- Confidentiality
- Demonstration copies
- Right to use copies
- Taxes
- Arbitration.

The rationales for these sections are the same as in a fixed-price agreement. In addition, a time-and-materials agreement will have a statement of location to tell where the work is to be performed and a statement that addresses the duration of the project.

Whether your agreement is on a fixed-price or time-and-materials basis, you'll want to avoid having your client send your agreement to the legal department for review. In most large corporations, this can delay the project start for months and may require you to engage an attorney as well. At some corporations, a legal review is unavoidable. But to avoid it wherever it's optional, remember to refer to your document as an agreement, never a contract. Make it simple and easy to understand. Don't try to hide anything or "put one over on" the client. If the client gets an uneasy feeling about the document, it will quickly go to the company's legal department.

Handling Changes

Once a client has decided to proceed with a project and work with you to complete it, your relationship is at an all-time high. It won't be that high again until the job is completely finished. When you bring up the subject of your agreement, take care not to "bring the client down." If you raise alarms in the client's mind, he or she may go with another resource. Say that you'll be sending the client a general agreement that you use for projects and that the company's representatives should feel comfortable about asking for any change that they believe is important.

When I hear from a client about changing an agreement that I've sent, I wear my best customer service hat and listen to them in spirit, as well in the words. I accept most changes that appear to be in good faith. If I don't agree with a proposed change, I explain why the statement is important to me or what my concerns are. Then the client and I may be able to come up with a compromise.

Remember that no matter what your agreement says, clients hold the trump cards. They have the money, and they have legal departments. If they want to, no matter what it says in your agreement, they can break you by keeping you in court. You need to be able to rely upon the good faith of the people you're working with. If they appear honest, give them whatever will make them comfortable. If they seem petty or dishonest and underhanded, walk away. You can't afford to do business with them, no matter how much you need money.

Drafting a Vendor/Client Agreement

If you think working with a client without a formal agreement is precarious, try working with an outside resource without an agreement. A good agreement with such outside resources as writers, programmers, or video producers contains many of the same elements of a client agreement except that now you are the client. Sections in a standard agreement with an outside resource should address the following:

- Deliverables
- Specifications
- Services (similar to scope of work)
- Payment
- Schedule
- Confidentiality
- Status
- Termination
- Arbitration
- Assumptions
- Ownership.

The information in these sections should be similar to that in your agreements with your clients, but you'll need to pay specific attention to how you draft the status, termination, assumptions, and ownership sections. When you prepare an agreement with an outside resource, address these issues as follows:

■ Status. Most training consulting firms make extensive use of independent contractors. Meanwhile federal and state governments are keeping close watch on businesses and industries that make extensive use of independent contractors (e.g., the motion picture industry). They believe that many of these folks should be kept or entered on company payrolls as employees.

To make sure that your associates know and understand that they're "outside" resources, you should make this explicit in your agreement. Stating this also will help if you are ever audited.

> **Example:** John Smith is an independent contractor to FT, not an employee, and is responsible for his own taxes.

■ Termination. You might think that people would know that if they're outside resources, they can be terminated at any time. But they may not know, or they may claim not to have realized this fact. Again, spelling out the situation will let your independent contractor know that you mean business, and having a written statement will come to your aid if a disagreement arises.

> **Example:** FT may cancel this agreement at any time.

■ Assumptions. Include all other information that you want to make sure that your resource knows and agrees to. This may include:

- when the person will be paid
- how the person represents him- or herself to your client (i.e., as a member of your company or as an independent resource)
- how long the person is to refrain from soliciting business from the client
- what happens if critical project deadlines are missed.

Example: FT will pay Jane Langer no later than 60 days after presentation of an invoice for completion of a valid milestone.

Jane Langer will not compete with FT or solicit training-related business from the Product Support Divisions of FCA for two years.

In the event that Jane Langer fails to meet any time frame set forth in this agreement, or any date subsequently agreed to, the amount due from FT shall be reduced by 20 percent for each week thereafter until the deliverable is received or the responsibility met.

■ Ownership. Professionals who do creative work (e.g., photographers and artists) like to retain rights to their work. Most clients feel that they should own 100 percent of work done for them and may believe that they can reuse any portion of it anytime in any way they want. But you cannot sell what you don't own in the first place. So be sure to get your outside resources to grant you complete ownership of the work that they complete. This will allow you to give your clients the reuse permission that they usually expect.

A sample of a complete agreement with an outside resource appears in the appendix at the end of this book.

Example: All rights to anything produced under this project are the sole property of FT and FCA. Under these rights, FCA may use and reproduce any and all portions of these deliverables without additional compensation to Jane Langer.

SECTION THREE: MAINTAINING AND EXPANDING YOUR PRACTICE

This section explains how to market yourself and your services, as well as how to capitalize on networking opportunities to maximize your visibility.

CHAPTER 9
Developing Sales and Marketing Materials

While many consultants spend a fortune trying to create slick and professional sales and marketing materials, large corporations spend even more to look homespun and personal. You can leapfrog the competition and save cash by creating personal, professional, sales and marketing materials with just a standard computer and laser printer.

Marketing With a Client Focus

Marketing materials are all the things that you use to communicate with clients and the people whom you'd like to have as your clients. But marketing itself requires much more than a slick brochure. In fact, a slick brochure usually is a waste of money for a training consultant who's just starting out. Marketing also requires more than sending out a newsletter twice a year or greeting cards during the holidays. It's a process that should be woven into everything you do.

I can't provide you all the information that you'll need to learn about developing an effective marketing program. Scores of books— some of which are listed at the end of this book—have been written about how to develop effective marketing materials and campaigns. Instead, I hope to give you a new way to look at marketing materials and how to use them to promote your training consulting practice.

Direct Mail and Advertising: What Works; What Doesn't

One of the most expensive mistakes I ever made was spending major money on a direct mail campaign. The mailing piece was great. The message was clear. The packaging was provocative. My mistake was in not noticing that no one searches the mailbox for information about companies that specialize in developing custom training courses that cost tens of thousands of dollars. Direct mail is fine for selling books and seminars, but if you're selling something that costs more than $1,000, direct mail won't get you far.

If you don't agree, check it out yourself: Ask one of your client's departmental assistants to show you where all the brochures and flyers that they get are kept. The assistant will show you a big box of everything that came in over the last couple of months. He or she will assure you that all of it will get looked at and filed somewhere, sometime, by some-one. Don't count on it, and don't spend your hard-earned money on sending out more of the same.

If, on the other hand, you want to promote a workshop and decide to use direct mail, consider this advice:

✔ **Don't make the information you send look like direct, or "junk" mail.**

Personalize the format. The most effective direct mail pieces look like letters from a friend.

✔ **Never lie or use fakey gimmicks.**

As I mentioned earlier, don't write PERSONAL on the envelope. Also avoid using a type font that looks like handwriting. People who pur-chase training consulting services are not stupid. They'll see through most lies and gimmicks immediately and will figure out the rest soon enough.

✔ **Avoid having your piece arrive on Monday, near a holiday, or during the summer.**

With the backlog of weekend mail, your piece will get lost in the Monday shuffle. For the same reason, time your direct mail arrivals to avoid the first few days after holidays. And speaking of holidays and vaca-tions, people's minds—and sometimes their bodies—are often out of the office during July and August, as well as from Thanksgiving to after New Year's, so avoid sending major promotions during these times of year.

✔ **Give people a reason to respond.**

Advertising, as honest people in that field will tell you, doesn't sell anything. It provides name recognition that, when coupled with an appropriate sales effort, leads to increased sales. If you're a well-financed training consulting firm that markets on-site workshops, advertising may increase the success of your sales representatives who call on corporate accounts. But don't expect to sell your workshops simply by running an ad (no mattered how well-placed) that gives your firm's (800) number.

To determine what your clients are most likely to open, reflect on what you do when you look through your mail. What do you look at, keep, or toss out? Chances are that you throw out the slick-looking stuff and open whatever looks like "real" mail (i.e., checks, bills, and letters from friends and business associates).

Forget about sending people marketing materials that look like checks or bills; that's sleazy and upsets people. But you honestly are a potential business associate and can send personalized letters to potential clients. (See sample letter of introduction on page 45.)

Getting Started: A Marketing Budget and Basic Materials

To make money, you're going to have to spend money. And you're going to have to spend it before you make it. If you find this reality hard to accept, you're not alone. But it's a fact. So set up a budget for marketing that you feel comfortable with and stick to it. Beyond the budget for developing your initial marketing materials, I recommend that your monthly budget include money to keep your marketing campaign going.

Your clients and prospective clients should hear from you once a month. What you send clients can vary, but let them hear from you frequently. For example, send an informative article that you published, a summary of a project that you recently completed, a newspaper or magazine article that you thought would be of interest, or a description of a new product or service that you're offering. Whatever you send, make sure the client perceives it as valuable, not just self-serving.

To get your marketing program started, you'll need a:

■ Capabilities brochure. Your capabilities brochure or handout should describe what your firm does, for whom, and what's so great about how you do it. Specifically, it should:

- Arouse people's curiosity.
- Tell them the benefits of what you'll be doing for them.
- Be personable.
- Show a sketch or small photograph of you.
- Avoid flashiness and "overselling."

■ Project list. You'll need a list that describes the projects that you've been involved with. (A sample project list appears in the appendix at the end of the book.) Organized by type of project (e.g., sales training or technical training), the descriptions should identify the "deliverables" that the client received (e.g., workbooks and videotapes) and the benefits of the project to the client—especially any "hard money" savings that they enjoyed. Stress any interesting or unique aspects of the project (e.g., that it was used by 15 audiences with members from 30 countries, who spoke 100 different languages).

■ **Collection of relevant articles or news items.** As previously noted, to demonstrate your capabilities and professionalism, you'll send professional contacts copies of articles that you wrote, articles about your work, news about the importance of training, or the benefits of a specific type of training that you do.

■ **A newsletter.** Keep your clients in mind when you read newspapers (especially the editorials) and professional journals and magazines. Some articles and items will be of interest to one or a handful of your clients and prospective clients. Others will have broad appeal; these will be the basis of your newsletter.

Most publications will let you reprint their articles in your newsletter if you ask for reprint permission. As a rule, they'll want a written request that names the publication and describes its readership.

Of course, you'll always keep your ears open for success stories about the work you've done with your clients. Think about asking a few of your most valued clients or professional associates to write articles for your newsletter. This gives them free exposure and publicity, and many will consider it an honor that you value their work enough to publish it. To develop an effective newsletter:

✔ **Know what you want to accomplish.**

Don't expect a newsletter to sell anything for you. While it may not put cash into your pocket immediately, a good newsletter may strengthen the loyalty of your customers, increase your visibility, elevate your company's image, and create client awareness of new applications of your products and services.

✔ **Plan your publication schedule carefully.**

Think about your clients' business cycles: When do your clients need training consulting services? At what trade shows do they introduce new products? When do they begin developing training programs for these new products? When do they select outside resources? When do your clients finalize their training budgets; at the beginning of the fiscal year or at the beginning of the calendar year? When do they start thinking about budgets, and when do they decide which programs and resources to use? Your answers to these questions will determine your publication schedule.

Research indicates that, in general, the best months for direct mail for training services are May and September, but I recommend that you coordinate your publication schedule with the business cycles of your clients. In scheduling your publication, be sure to:

- Reach people at the right time—when they are seriously considering training consulting resources, not before and surely not after.
- Schedule six to eight weeks for producing and mailing your newsletter.
- Give the reader value.

A newsletter is not a multiple-page advertisement. Your customers will only read your newsletter if it contains information that they believe is of value to them. Include articles that are of general interest to people involved with training, such as tips and techniques, state-of-the art methods and media, and success stories from companies that have used training to accomplish strategic corporate objectives.

■ **Folder.** You'll need an attractive folder to put your capabilities brochure, project list, and newsletters into for presentation or mailing to clients.

The first time that you speak with a prospective client over the telephone, you're usually asked to send them "something." Many consultants will offer to fax material "now" and call back "this" afternoon. I find that's too rushed for most people. Of course, you should be prepared to fax your capabilities brochure if it's the client who is intent on speed.

Most of the time, though, if you believe that a prospect is serious, send the potential client all of the information that you have—capabilities brochure, project list, articles, newsletters, etc.—packaged in a coordinated folder. You can buy folders in a variety of styles and paper stocks at your local office-supply superstore or through such catalogues as Paper Direct. If you want your firm's name and address on the folders, be prepared to pay much more. You can order printed folders through a local full-service printer or copy shop.

As I've said earlier, if you suspect that a prospect isn't serious and only asked you to send something to get you off the phone, simply send a general one- to two-page letter in a business envelope.

■ Capabilities presentation. A capabilities presentation includes the materials that you use to introduce yourself and your firm during introductory meetings with client representatives. You may use a few slides to support a 15-minute presentation that covers who you are, what you do, the benefits of what you do, what companies you've done it for, how you do it, and what makes you better than any other training consultant in the world.

Capabilities presentations on overheads used to be fine, but not anymore. I recommend that you use professional looking slides for large audiences and 8-by-10-inch pictures of those slides in a freestanding binder for small audiences. Better yet, put the whole presentation on a lap-top computer, bring your own display device, and watch those bullets dance around the screen. Today's business people are technology-oriented and really love those dancing bullets.

Striving To Be Distinctively Different

When you see a print advertisement that's positively ingenious, set it aside. Keep a file of ads that grabbed your attention, made you smile, or nod in agreement. Refer to this file when you're creating your next advertising or marketing piece.

I admired the advertising of training services that the Pacific Group did. One ad had a picture of a red-cheeked good-old-boy with a large hammer that took up most of the ad space. The caption read: "When you have a hammer, every problem needs pounding." The ad copy went on to say that most training companies use cookie-cutter solutions but the Pacific Group takes unique and creative approaches toward training. I believed this message, because the ad itself showed creativity. The

Pacific Group combined a picture, a strong message, and great creativity to present an effective advertisement.

The advertisement described above was different from any other advertisement for a training consulting company that I had ever seen. It was defiantly different, and that's why it was so memorable. You too should strive to be distinctively different in every aspect of the marketing of your professional practice. You don't have the money to use the so-called tried-and-true techniques, and they don't work very well for consultants anyway. Clients don't want consultants who offer more of the same. If they wanted the "same," they could do it themselves. They want "different."

Projecting the Right Image

Everything that you send to a client or prospect should reflect how you want them to think of you. Your style might be professional, with a capital "P", arty, or tastefully creative. Your image should be consistent with what you do. Clients expect an organizational development consultant to be a "suit," a video production consultant to be arty, and a trainer to be somewhere in between.

Whatever your image is, project it in every aspect of your newsletter, including the writing style, graphics, typography, and even the paper. As Einstein said, "God is in the details."

CHAPTER 10
Getting Repeat Business

Research by a leading training company showed that clients won't necessarily give their repeat business to training consulting firms that they're satisfied with. They won't necessarily give their repeat business to training consulting firms that they're pleased with either.

They will only automatically give repeat business to training consulting firms that leave them "dancing in the streets." Let that phrase sink in: "dancing in the streets." If you want to show your face in your clients' offices again, that's the standard you may have to meet.

Working With People

You may think that you're working with the FCA company, but you really aren't. You're working with Tina, Jim, and Joan. Never forget that you're working with people—people who have hopes, wishes, and dreams. People who probably are living work lives that are smaller than they are. People who have families and other interests outside of work. People who have good days and bad.

As representatives of FCA Inc., their primary expectation is to get the services and products contracted for in a project, but they also hope to get something personal for their efforts—perhaps a promotion, recognition, or new skills. And they always hope for respectful, pleasant working relationships.

No matter who you're working with on a project, you need to remember that client representatives are employees of the company and you're not. No matter how important you think you are, and despite your degrees and 20 years of experience, it would be much easier to terminate you than to fire them. If you ever want to work in a place again, you need to treat every client-employee like gold.

Without doubt, the strongest fear that clients have about consultants is that they will not be able to control them. Clients are more afraid of hiring a "loose cannon" than of hiring an incompetent consultant. So during each and every project phase, take care to let client representatives know that you are working for them and that they are in control. As with many things in life, perception is everything. The fact that you may

have far more expertise in your field than the client representatives have is irrelevant. What's important is that they feel comfortable. Be humble about your credentials, defer to the client representatives' better judgment because of their knowledge and understanding of their organization, and thank them for the expertise that they share with you.

Setting Expectations and Being Flexible

In his book *Flawless Consulting*,[3] Peter Block talks about the importance of being candid with your clients about what they can expect of you and what you expect from them. He also discusses consultants' natural inclination to avoid discussing their own expectations and needs for fear that revealing these may "blow the project." Yes, some clients expect or would like consultants to be able to complete projects without any involvement on their part. Conversely, a few clients expect to direct even the smallest of activities. But "good" clients understand that successful project completion typically involves a measure of trust and much collaboration. It's best to set expectations early on—to discuss what the consultant and client representatives expect of each other on the business and personal levels. This is how to plan for success.

But, despite the best of plans, "stuff" happens; stuff that neither you nor clients could have foreseen. The consultants whose clients are "dancing in the streets" realize that a good relationship requires flexibility from all involved. They also know that the person who has to be flexible first is the one who is being paid the big bucks.

Giving Something More

Doing a job done well is no longer enough to ensure that you'll get repeat business. To leave your clients "dancing in the streets" with delight, you'll have to give them something more. I can't tell you exactly what that "something" will be; it will depend on the client and the project. It could be that you'll be flexible about their need to move the schedule forward a couple of weeks. It could be that you'll agree to revise a training module that they had already approved. It could be that you'll repeat a pilot test at your own expense because the client recruited the wrong students.

In today's competitive environment, clients expect more than a narrow interpretation of their agreement with you. If you don't offer "something more," the next time that they plan a new project, they'll call your competitors as well as (or instead of) you.

Sharing Credit

Many consultants speak of successful projects as if their efforts alone created the success. No one person can create a successful project; at least several people's skills and efforts are needed. And, as I've said, successful projects almost always reflect good work on the part of the client, as well as the consultant and his or her associates. Give credit where credit is due and give it often. Acknowledge the role and contributions of client representatives and your firm's associates.

Expanding Your Client Base

Many consultants are happy to have a few good clients, but their complacency is risky. Companies are acquired or go out of business, divisions move, and people change jobs. In short, a good client today may be gone tomorrow. For decades, the rule of thumb was that a client list would "turn over" 100 percent every 10 years. Now it's probably quicker.

Please take this cautionary tale to heart: Once I had a steady client that provided more than half of my business. The client was a large company with many divisions, a great referral network, and lots of money. Then things changed. The company stopped doing so well, and it offered employees early retirement. One of my best contacts and sources of referral took that retirement option and became my competitor. I haven't seen a penny of the company's money for years.

I'd always known that this could happen, but I didn't expect it to happen so quickly. I didn't even recognize that the loss probably was permanent until months after it happened. Fortunately, I had the good sense to market my firm even while I was feasting on my "Number One." I was able to pull out of it. Training consulting firms that don't invest in steady marketing often aren't as lucky.

Ask a few training consultants what they dislike most about being working for themselves. Many will tell you that its the peaks and valleys that I mentioned in Chapter 1. While engaged in a project, consultants may work day and night. When the project is over, they are unemployed, often for months at a stretch. Some consultants call this the "valley of death." I've been through it more than once, and it's not pretty.

To succeed as a training consultant, you need to stay in touch with the professional contacts that you already have and to reach out to make new ones on a regular basis. Marketing is an investment, not an overnight miracle. You may not see any results after a week or several months. It's like planting and watering seeds: have patience, keep at it, and results will surface and eventually blossom.

Marketing "in between" projects is too haphazard. What's more, you should aim to reduce the time that you spend between projects to practically no time. So whether you're working on a project or not, commit to dutifully working at activities to build your practice at least one day a week. When I recommend spending a full day a week on sales and marketing activities, I don't mean that as a rough guide. I mean it literally. In my opinion, a half-day isn't enough and two days every couple of weeks isn't equivalent. I advise working on marketing on the same day each week, every week of the year for the rest of your consulting life. It's your ticket to success. Make this investment in marketing consistently, and you'll reap financial and personal rewards that make your investment of time, money, and effort well worthwhile.

The day will come when you get a telephone call out of the blue from someone who'd like you to do a project or speak at a conference. This may be someone that you've never spoken to before, much less had the pleasure of meeting. When that happens, pat yourself on the back and say a little prayer of thanks that your marketing is finally working.

Critical Marketing Activities

A day a week may sound like a lot to you, but if you look at the valleys of death you may have over the period of a year, you may spend 20 percent of your time unemployed anyway. Why not spend it proactively avoiding future valleys instead of just pulling yourself out of your latest one. Start your marketing efforts by concentrating on a few critical marketing activities.

Calling people is just the beginning. In fact, most marketing professionals wouldn't consider making telephone calls to be marketing. They'd call that "sales." I'll leave the technical differences between sales and marketing to the professionals in those fields. To me, the major difference lies in the timing of the expected payoff. When you're performing sales activities, you're looking for an immediate payoff (such as a having a face-to-face meeting or receiving a signed agreement within two weeks). The investment in marketing activities, on the other hand, is long-term. Such activities don't pay off in immediate sales, but make you and your services known to people who can give you business in the future.

So make telephone sales calls whenever you learn of a potential client or a possible project with a current or former client. And continue marketing your firm through the activities that brought you into the consulting world: writing, speaking, being active in professional organizations, and networking with other training consultants.

Giving Something Back: Favors and Community Service

A former boss of mine (from the deep South) was fond of saying, "I don't mind being a pig, but I'd never want to be a hog because pigs get fat and hogs get slaughtered."

People don't want to work with someone who's a non-stop taker: Takers flaunt wealth, feel and act superior to everyone else, and want nothing to do with the people who helped them get to where they are today. Takers are hogs and, ultimately, most get what's coming to them.

When you start your practice, your professional contacts, both associates and clients, will want to see you succeed as a training consultant. Everyone likes to know people who have done well. If you follow the recommendations of this book, you'll probably do well—which puts you in a position to start acting like a hog. But remember the words of my wise, former boss: Pigs are okay; hogs, never.

The best way to continue to succeed as consultant is to give something back to everyone who helped you along the way. Tom Hopkins, a well-known sales trainer, explains this as a "favor bank."[4] Whenever you do someone a favor, you're making a deposit in this bank. Whenever you ask a favor from someone, you're making a withdrawal. Hopkins advises that you keep the balances in all of your favor banks well on the plus side.

No matter how talented you are as a training consultant or how skilled at sales, you simply can't succeed as a consultant without the help of others. You depend on other people's continued business, referrals, advice, and high regard for you. So acknowledge and pay back favors. Better yet, don't always wait until you've made a withdrawal from the favor bank before you make a deposit. Start a "savings" plan. Look for opportunities to do favors for people, and do these favors with an open heart. Don't expect to be reimbursed directly or immediately.

Thinking in terms of Hopkins's favor bank may change how you act in other ways. For example, many consultants take referrals for granted. They believe that if they've done a good job for someone, that person has an obligation to serve as a reference until the end of time. But people have other pressing things to do, so when you ask a client representative to serve as a reference for your firm, you're asking for a favor. Be prepared to return the favor—quickly. Send the client representative a thank-you card as soon as he or she agrees to be a reference. If you get a project partly because of a client reference, send the client representative a basket of fruit or flowers and another thank-you. This kind of behavior will keep your favor bank full.

A wonderful way to "give something back" is to provide your expertise pro bono (which means without pay) to community organizations. No matter what you do or where your heart is, there's a community organization that needs your help but can't pay for it. I recommend that you first consider helping the community organizations that you're already affiliated with: the place where you worship; the community centers and civic groups that you attend; the senior-citizens' community where your mom lives; or your children's schools. All of these places can benefit from your expertise as a training consultant. They may not need for you to do training itself, but they probably can use your interviewing, planning, or management skills.

I once enjoyed being a member of the strategic planning committee for a community center. In addition to providing input into the process, I helped the committee develop questionnaires and conducted several focus groups.

Once you've tried your wings out on smaller projects for community organizations, I recommend that you look for larger projects to take on as part of your active involvement in professional associations. Marketing in this manner will make you feel good as you "do good" for the training profession.

Community outreach activities not only warm your heart, they may pay you back monetarily as well. Perhaps an organization that you've donated time to will decide to pay you to continue your work or to do more. Perhaps another organization that you've had contact with through your volunteer efforts, or that has heard of your fine work, will offer you a paid project.

Don't let your good deeds go unnoticed. Publicize your community work and it will reap dividends for your cause and your firm. Perhaps you'll be featured in a newspaper article or be interviewed for a local or national television show. It could happen, you know.

I have been a training consultant for all of my adult life. As of the date of this writing, I have headed my own training consulting firm for 12 of those years. In what seems to be a lifetime, I have probably made every mistake in the book. My sincerest wish is that I have saved you from some of these.

Happy trails!

REFERENCES

[1] *The Professional Consultant & Seminar Business Report,* May 1988.

[2] Block, Peter. *Flawless Consulting: A Guide To Getting Your Expertise Used.* San Diego: Pfeiffer & Company, 1981.

[3] Block, Peter. *Flawless Consulting: A Guide To Getting Your Expertise Used.* San Diego: Pfeiffer & Company, 1981.

[4] Hopkins, Tom. *How To Master the Art of Selling.* New York: Warner Books, 1982.

RECOMMENDED RESOURCES

Professional Organizations

Suggestions for Further Reading

Professional Organizations

The telephone numbers listed below were correct at press time, but may change. For more information about these groups and their publications and conferences, see the current edition of the *Encyclopedia of Associations* (published by Gale Research), which is available in the reference sections of many public and college libraries.

American Society for Healthcare Education & Training
American Hospital Association
840 N. Lakeshore Drive
Chicago, IL 60611
312/280-3556

American Management Association
135 West 50th Street
New York, NY 10020
212/586-8100

American Society for Quality Control
611 East Wisconsin Avenue
Post Office Box 3005
Milwaukee, WI 53201-3005
414/272-8575

Association for Multi-Image International
10008 North Dale Mabry
Suite 113
Tampa, FL 33618
813/960-1692

Association for Quality and Participation
801-B West 8th Street
Suite 501
Cincinnati, OH 45203-1601
513/381-1959

Human Resource Planning Society
401 East 42nd Street
Suite 1509
New York, NY 10017
212/490-6387

International Customer Service Association
401 North Michigan Avenue
Chicago, IL 60611-4267
312/321-6800

International TV Association
6311 North O'Connor Road
LB 51
Irving, TX 75039
214/869-1112

Meeting Planners International
1950 Stemmons Freeway
Infomart Building
Suite 5018
Dallas, TX 75207
214/712-7702

National Society for Performance and Instruction
1300 L Street, NW
Suite 1250
Washington, DC 20005
202/408-7969

National Staff Development Council
Post Office Box 240
Oxford, OH 45056
513/523-6029

Organizational Development Network
Post Office 69329
Portland, OR 97201
503/246-0148

Professional Society for Sales and Marketing Trainers
(formerly National Society of Sales Training Executives)
1900 Arch Street
Philadelphia, PA 19103-1498
215/564-3484

Society for Applied Learning Technology
50 Culpeper Street
Warrenton, VA 22186
703/347-0055

Society for Technical Communication
901 North Stuart Street
Suite 904
Arlington, VA 22203
703/522-4114

Suggestions for Further Reading

The print materials listed below may be purchased through their publishers. Those marked with asterisks also may be purchased through the American Society for Training and Development (at a discount to National ASTD members).

Books & Booklets

*Arrendondo, Lani. *How to Present Like a Pro*. New York: McGraw-Hill, 1991.

*Bedrosian, Maggie. *INFO-LINE: How To Make a Large Group Presentation*. Alexandria, VA: American Society for Training and Development, February 1991.

*Bellman, Geoffrey M. *The Consultant's Calling*. San Francisco: Jossey-Bass, 1990.

Block, Peter. *Flawless Consulting: A Guide To Getting Your Expertise Used*. San Diego: Pfeiffer & Company, 1981.

*Callahan, Madelyn R., ed. *INFO-LINE: How To Market Your Training Programs*. Alexandria, VA: American Society for Training and Development, 1986.

*Callahan, Madelyn. *INFO-LINE: Make Every Presentation a Winner*. Alexandria, VA: American Society for Training and Development, June 1986.

*Callahan, Madelyn. *INFO-LINE: Be a Better Writer*. Alexandria, VA: American Society for Training and Development, November 1986.

*Corrigan, Marilyn and Sparhawk, Sally. *INFO-LINE: Becoming an Outside Consultant*. Alexandria, VA: American Society for Training and Development, April 1993.

*Darraugh, Barbara, ed. *INFO-LINE: Organizational Culture*. Alexandria, VA: American Society for Training and Development, April 1993.

Edwards, Paul & Sarah; Clampitt Douglas, Laura. *Getting Business To Come to You*. New York: Jeremy P. Tarcher/Perigee Books, 1990.

Edwards, Paul & Sarah. *Making It on Your Own*. New York: Jeremy P. Tarcher/Perigee Books, 1991.

Edwards, Paul & Sarah. *Working From Home (rev.).* New York: Jeremy P. Tarcher/Perigee Books, 1994.

Greenbaum, Thomas L. *The Consultants Manual: A Complete Guide To Building a Successful Consulting Practice.* New York: John Wiley & Sons, 1990.

Hopkins, Tom. *How To Master the Art of Selling.* New York: Warner Books, 1982.

Johnson, Barbara L. *Private Consulting: How To Turn Experience Into Employment Dollars.* Englewood Cliffs, NJ: Prentice-Hall, 1982.

*Kirrane, Diane E. *INFO-LINE: Be a Better Speaker.* Alexandria, VA: American Society for Training and Development, February 1988.

*Malouf, Doug. *How To Create and Deliver a Dynamic Presentation.* Alexandria, VA: American Society for Training and Development, 1993.

*Metzger, Robert O. *Profitable Consulting: Guiding America's Managers into the Next Century.* Reading, MA: Addison-Wesley, 1989.

*Meyer, Kathy M. *INFO-LINE: Coming to Agreement: How To Resolve Conflict.* Alexandria, VA: American Society for Training and Development, September 1989.

*Poore, Jerry and Larry Lottier. *INFO-LINE: Ethics for Business.* Alexandria, VA: American Society for Training and Development, March 1991.

Robinson, Dan G.; Younglove, Bob. *Making Your Career Transition into External HRD Consulting.* Alexandria, VA: American Society for Training and Development, 1986.

Schrello, Don M. *How To Market Training Programs, Seminars, and Instructional Materials.* Long Beach, CA: Schrello Direct Marketing, 1985.

Shenson, Howard L. *The Contract and Fee-Setting Guide for Consultants and Professionals.* New York, NY: John Wiley & Sons, 1990.

Tepper, Ron. *Become a Top Consultant: How the Experts Do It.* New York: John Wiley & Sons, 1985.

Weiss, Alan. *Million Dollar Consulting: The Professional's Guide To Growing a Practice.* New York, NY: McGraw-Hill, 1992.

Articles

Montgomery, Daniel J.; Vogt, Judith F. and Pincus, Laura B. "Process Consulting: Legal and Relational Considerations in Developing Consultant-Client Contracts." *Organization Development Journal,* Spring 1993, vol. 11, no. 1, pp. 23-30.

*Petrini, Catherine M., ed. "Putting a Price on Your Head." *Training & Development,* July 1990, vol. 47, no. 7, pp.15-22.

Newsletters and Magazines

Home Office Computing
(Scholastic, Inc.)
P.O. Box 2511
Boulder, CO 80302
800/288-7812

Performance Improvement Quarterly
Learning Systems Institute
Florida State University
919 W. College R-19
Florida State University
Tallahassee, FL 32306

Performance & Instruction
National Society for Performance & Instruction
1300 L Street, NW.
Suite 1250
Washington, DC 20005
202/408-7969

Training & Development
American Society for Training and Development
1640 King Street
Box 1443
Alexandria, VA 22313-2043
703/683-8100

Training Director's Forum
Lakewood Publications
50 S. Ninth St.
Minneapolis, MN 55402
800/328-4329

Training
Lakewood Publications
50 S. Ninth St.
Minneapolis, MN 55402
800/328-4329

APPENDIX: Samples

Fixed-Price Design and Development Agreement

Fixed-Price Workshop Agreement

General Time-and-Materials Agreement

Agreement with an Outside Resource

Sample Project List

About the Author

Fixed-Price Design and Development Agreement

1. SCOPE OF WORK AND SCHEDULE
Design, develop, and produce self-paced training course to train employees to enter information and analyze reports produced by, or within, TRACKS. This course will be separated into three parts and take up to 5 hours for students to complete.

Materials for this course will include a tutorial and mastery test of up to 120 (8.5-by-6.75 inches) pages, 15 simple illustrations or flow charts, and a data diskette with sample data.

FCA will provide FT with camera-ready copies of any screens required.

Should FCA fail to meet, or cause FT to fail to meet, the time frames on this schedule, FT may alter the dates for completing remaining milestones based upon the availability of its resources at that time.

2. SECURITY INTEREST
FT retains a security interest in all such items until the purchase price has been paid in full.

3. PAYMENT
FT will be paid $25,000 according to the following payment schedule:

Project start up	25%
Delivery of design	15%
Approval of design	15%
Delivery of drafts	15%
Approval of drafts	15%
Delivery of produced masters	15%

4. TERMINATION
Either party may cancel this agreement with two weeks written notice. If FT cancels the agreement, it must provide FCA with copies of materials corresponding to all project milestones that FCA has paid for.

If FCA cancels this agreement, FCA must pay for all milestones complet-

ed and approved, as well as for any additional work completed on a
time-and-materials basis according to FT's standard billing rates.

If FCA cancels this workshop within one week of the implementation
date, FCA and FT may reschedule the workshop to a mutually convenient date. If FCA provides less than one week's notice, FCA is responsible for payment in full.

5. PROJECT REVIEW POINTS
The FCA representative having authority to approve and sign off on all
review and authorization points in this project shall be Chris Harris.

FCA shall expeditiously review material submitted at each review point
by FT. Any costs associated with FCA changes subsequent to FCA written
approval of a particular review point shall be borne by FCA.

6. SALES-AND-USE TAXES
FCA shall be responsible for and will pay all applicable sales-and-use
taxes directly to FT. FCA also will pay any additional taxes upon submis-
sion of a bill from appropriate tax authorities.

7. FCA SHALL AID THE PROGRAM DEVELOPMENT ACTIVITIES BY:
a. Providing reasonable and timely access to all facilities, equipment,
   and people for purposes of research and review
b. Providing correct and timely information to include course outlines
   and manuals relevant to the subject matter of the program
c. Assigning a project manager to coordinate the gathering of information and review of materials
d. Providing subject-matter experts and representatives of the target
   training audience as required for information gathering, review, and
   testing
e. Reviewing materials in a timely manner
f. Providing four to eight personnel who meet the course entry requirements, and facilities for testing of the training program
g. Adhering to the schedule identified in the proposal or any mutually
   agreeable revised schedule with respect to reviewing and approving
   major review points and supplying of any required materials

8. REIMBURSED EXPENSES

FCA shall reimburse FT for the following expenses in connection with this project:

a. Travel expenses to include air fare, local transportation, lodging, and meals

b. Telephone expenditures

c. Postage, copying, and freight/shipping expenses

9. DELAYS

FT shall not be liable for delays caused by FCA. Neither FT nor FCA shall be liable for delays in delivery or failure to produce due to natural disasters, including but not limited to, fires, floods, earthquakes, strikes, or civil disturbances.

10. DEMONSTRATION COPIES

FT shall be provided with two (2) complete reproduced copies of all deliverables under this agreement.

11. RIGHT TO USE COPIES

FT shall be allowed to use nonconfidential portions of demonstration copies for internal applications, capabilities demonstrations, and sales promotion purposes upon written approval by FCA.

12. CONFIDENTIALITY

FT agrees that the subject matter of the services provided to FCA shall be confidential and, therefore, FT will not disclose such information to any third party.

13. ARBITRATION

Any dispute or controversy arising under or in connection with this agreement shall be settled exclusively by arbitration in [city, state] in accordance with the rules of the American Arbitration Association in effect at the time. Judgment may be entered on the arbitrator's award in any court having jurisdiction. All costs for such arbitration, as well as any attorney fees and costs incurred in enforcing this agreement, will be paid by the prevailing party.

14. INITIAL SCHEDULE

Information gathering	4/20–4/24
(Interviews)	4/23–4/25
FT creates design document	4/27–5/5
FCA reviews design document	5/6–5/10
FCA/FT review design document	5/11
FT revises design document	5/12
FCA approves design document	5/13
FT develops drafts	5/14–6/10
FCA reviews drafts	6/11–6/16
FCA/FT review drafts	6/17
FCA approves drafts	
FT revision of drafts	6/18–6/25
FCA/FT pilot test	6/26
FT produces camera-ready materials	6/29–7/13

ACCEPTED BY:

FCA	FT
Name: Mr. Chris Harris	Dr. Joel Gendelman
Signature:_____	_____
Title: _____	Senior Partner
Date: _____	_____

Fixed-Price Workshop Agreement

1. SCOPE OF WORK
FT will present two, two-hour runnings of the workshop, Dullbusters: Building Excitement with Activity-Based Training on December 2, 1995. This workshop will be presented by Dr. Joel Gendelman.

2. COPYRIGHT
All materials are copyrighted by FT. BUYER personnel may use those copies provided to them by FT. Additional copies or the right to make additional copies must be negotiated separately with FT.

3. PAYMENT
BUYER agrees to pay FT $5,000.

4. EXPENSES
BUYER will arrange and pay for all travel arrangements, including airfare, food, lodging, and transportation. BUYER will reimburse FT for incidental travel expenses.

BUYER will reproduce, or pay for, the reproduction of all handouts.

BUYER shall pay:

- $2,500 as a nonrefundable deposit, upon signing this agreement
- $2,500 the day of the workshop
- Reimbursement of travel expenses within 15 days of presentation of the workshop

5. RESCHEDULING
BUYER may reschedule this workshop to a mutually convenient time with 14 days of advance written notice.

ACCEPTED BY:

BUYER	FT
Name: Ms. Jo Thorn	Dr. Joel Gendelman
Signature:_____	_____
Title: National Training Director	Senior Partner
Date: _____	_____

General Time-and-Materials Agreement

1. SCOPE OF WORK

FT will provide FCA with training consulting services on the design and development of training for project Horizon.

2. PAYMENT

FT's fee structure is as follows:

- Senior Staff Member $100 per hour
- Instructional Designer/
  Production Assistant $75 per hour
- Clerical Support $35 per hour
- Outside Purchases   Cost plus 15 percent

Moderate travel on full working days will not be charged. Travel on non-full working days will be charged at 50 percent.

Copying, long distance communication, travel, mileage, and shipping charges will be billed separately.

FT will submit bi-weekly invoices identifying the days worked and expenses incurred. FCA will promptly pay FT within 15 days of receipt of invoice.

FT will require a retainer of $1,500 to begin this project.

3. CLIENT RESPONSIBILITIES

FCA will provide FT with written information, verbal information, and equipment as it is required for successful performance of this project.

4. LOCATION

The services covered under this agreement will be performed at FT in West Hills, California.

5. DURATION

This agreement shall last until modified or canceled in writing.

6. CONFIDENTIALITY

FT agrees and promises that the subject matter of its services provided to FCA shall be held to be confidential and to not disclose such information to any third party.

7. DEMONSTRATION COPIES

FCA shall provide FT with two (2) complete reproduced copies of all materials developed under this agreement.

8. RIGHT TO USE COPIES

FT shall be allowed to use nonconfidential portions of demonstration copies for internal applications, capabilities demonstrations, and sales promotion purposes upon written approval by FCA.

9. TAXES

FCA will be responsible for all applicable sales-and-use taxes and pay any additional taxes when presented with notification from appropriate taxation authorities.

10. ARBITRATION

Any dispute or controversy arising under or in connection with this Agreement shall be settled exclusively by arbitration in [city, state] in accordance with the rules of the American Arbitration Association then in effect. Judgment may be entered on the arbitrator's award in any court having jurisdiction. FCA agrees to pay all costs for such arbitration, as well as any attorney fees and costs incurred in enforcing this agreement.

Name: Mr. Chris Harris   Dr. Joel Gendelman
Signature:_____   _____
Title: _____   Senior Partner
Date: _____   _____

Agreement With an Outside Resource

1. DELIVERABLES

- Scripts for two videos (10 minutes each)
- Fully-produced audio masters shot on 1-inch or Sony Beta cam
- Masters with a separate audio version

2. SPECIFICATIONS

- Each video presentation up to 10 minutes running time
- Each video will correspond to approved treatments in the Course Design Document (attached)
- Each video will include three actors, one of whom also will be used as an off-camera narrator
- Vendor will bear all travel and production costs
- Each video will match the production quality and style of the attached sample

3. SERVICES
The services performed by Jane Langer will include performing the following to FT's satisfaction.

- Develop the script
- Revise the script as per FT's specifications
- Review the script with FCA
- Revise the script as per FCA's specifications
- Fully produce the two presentations
- Revise the produced presentations as per FT's specifications
- Revise the produced presentations as per FCA's specifications

4. PAYMENT
FT will pay Jane Langer the sum of $10,000.
The above payment will be made according to the following FT approved milestones.

FT's script approval	$2,500
FCA's script approval	$2,500
FT's approval of produced masters	$2,500
Delivery of FCA approved produced masters	$2,500

5. SCHEDULE

Develop the script	7/25–8/1
Revise the script as per FT's specifications	8/5–8/6
Review the script with FCA	8/16
Revise the script per FCA's specifications	8/19
Fully produce the two presentations	8/27–9/4
Revise the produced presentations as per FCA's specifications	9/12–9/13

6. CONFIDENTIALITY

As an associate of FT, Jane Langer agrees to keep all material and information provided to me by FT or its client confidential and secure. She will not divulge any information regarding FT, its clients, or the projects that she is assigned to without prior written permission from FT. She also agrees to keep confidential and not show or demonstrate any materials developed under contract with FT without prior written permission from FT.

7. STATUS

Jane Langer is an independent contractor to FT, not an employee, and is responsible for her own taxes, etc.

8. TERMINATION

FT may cancel this agreement at any time.

9. ARBITRATION

Any dispute or controversy arising under or in connection with this Agreement shall be settled exclusively by arbitration in [city, state] in accordance with the rules of the American Arbitration Association then in effect. Judgment may be entered on the arbitrator's award in any court having jurisdiction. The prevailing party will pay all costs for such arbitration, as well as any attorney fees and costs incurred in enforcing this agreement.

10. ASSUMPTIONS

Jane Langer will not compete with FT or solicit training-related business from the Product Support Division of FCA for two years.

In the event that Jane Langer fails to meet any time frame set forth in this agreement, or any date subsequently agreed to, the amount due from FT shall be reduced by 20 percent for each week thereafter until the deliverable is received or responsibility met.

11. OWNERSHIP

All rights to anything produced under this project are the sole property of FT and FCA. Under these rights, FCA may use and reproduce any and all portions of these deliverables without additional compensation to Jane Langer.

Name: _____   Dr. Joel Gendelman

Signature:_____   _____

Title: _____   Senior Partner

Date: _____   _____

Sample Project List

- ■ Computer-Based and Multimedia
- • Multimedia course to train automobile technicians to troubleshoot electronic problems
- • Computer-Based Training program to train a variety of audiences to gather and use quality control data
- • Self-study curriculum for financial analysts and accountants to train them to use a worldwide financial reporting system
- • Self-study and computer interactive training program to train a variety of office personnel to use a sophisticated computer communications service

- ■ Sales
- • Workshop to train several levels of resellers to sell data communications products
- • Media-based course to train dealers to sell a complete peripherals product line
- • Marketing guides for high-technology sales representatives
- • Workshop to train resellers to sell a network operating system
- • Workshop to train members of several sales channels to sell a line of network products
- • Series of courses to train platform officers and branch managers to sell a new investment product

- ■ Computer Applications
- • Workshop training course to train third-party support personnel to effectively support OS/2
- • Self-study curriculum to train accountants and bookkeepers to use a commercial accounting system
- • Comprehensive documentation system to train office manager and office staff to set-up, use, and maintain a pervasive computerized medical management system

■ Technical
- Workshop to train customer MIS personnel to plan and design complex networks
- Hands-on course to train customer engineers to install, configure, verify and problem identify network products using standard tools
- Training study and curriculum plan to train field engineers to repair computer peripheral products
- Corporate-wide needs analysis and curriculum design for the technical training of telecommunications sales, support, and customer personnel

ABOUT THE AUTHOR

Joel Gendelman is a recognized authority on training, performance improvement, and the marketing of consulting services. He is Senior Partner of Future Technologies, located in Littleton, Colorado. Joel's clients include Intel, Nissan, Hewlett-Packard, and Microsoft. Joel has served as the President of the Los Angeles Chapter of the National Society for Performance and Instruction (NSPI), a member of the Editorial Boad of *Performance & Instruction*, and Director of Marketing for the Los Angeles Chapter of the American Society for Training and Development. He is currently a member of the Board of Directors of the Rocky Mountain Chapter of NSPI. Dr. Gendelman has published over 50 entertaining articles, appeared on both radio and television programs, and is a sought after speaker to Fortune 100 companies and professional societies.

Joel holds a bachelor's degree from the State University of New York at Stony Brook, as well as a master's and doctorate from the Catholic University of America in Washington, D.C.